Persian Gi

This is a book for reference and revision, aimed at those in the early stages of studying the Persian language. It uses the official reformed spelling, and covers handwriting, educated standard and educated colloquial pronunciation, as well as the important polite forms. The grammar is explained with numerous examples that are given in both Persian script and Roman transcription. Grammatical themes are grouped logically, and there are cross-references, appendices and a subject index to facilitate the search for the right form.

John Mace has worked in the Diplomatic Service, as a British Council lecturer in Iran, as a personnel officer in the Middle East and as a European Commission Delegate. He has written Persian, Arabic and German language manuals, and a verse translation of Russian poetry.

PERSIAN GRAMMAR

For reference and revision

John Mace

RoutledgeCurzon
Taylor & Francis Group
LONDON AND NEW YORK

First published 2003
by RoutledgeCurzon
2 Park Square, Milton Park, Abingdon, Oxon OX14 4RN

Simultaneously published in the USA and Canada
by RoutledgeCurzon
270 Madison Ave, New York, NY 10016

RoutledgeCurzon is an imprint of the Taylor & Francis Group

Reprinted 2004, 2005 (twice)

Prepared and typeset by John Mace
Printed and bound in Great Britain by
St Edmundsbury Press Ltd, Bury St Edmunds, Suffolk

British Library Cataloguing in Publication Data
A catalogue record is available for this book from the British Library

Library of Congress Cataloguing in Publication Data
A catalogue record for this book has been requested

ISBN 0–700–71694–7 (hbk)
ISBN 0–700–71695–5 (pbk)

Contents

Contents

Contents

Contents

Contents

Introduction

This is a revision and reference grammar book whose purpose is to act as support for any course of Persian, and especially to help students in their early and intermediate stages.

It is not a course book. Each paragraph makes as few assumptions as possible about previous knowledge of the theme being studied. The book does not claim to examine every point in the language, merely to cover the most practical ones.

Maximum advantage has been taken of the fact that Persian has an Indo-European grammatical structure, familiar to most Europeans.

Although the book follows modern spelling, it indicates also those older forms of spelling still found today.

The transcription accompanying the Persian script is an accurate reflection of the pronunciation. Educated colloquial variants of the standard pronunciation are shown and explained; this colloquial pronunciation is socially completely 'correct', and you are recommended to use it whenever you are not reading aloud or quoting from a written text. Standard pronunciation is always acceptable; but without a knowledge of colloquial pronunciation you will miss much of what is said to you; and your own spoken Persian will never 'take off' without at least some use of it. Colloquial forms are shown in angular quotation marks ‹ › in the transcription.

Grammar books sometimes separate much information into morphology (word structure) and syntax (sentence structure). Many students find this distinction unnecessary. In this book, points of syntax are, as far as possible, studied together with the appropriate parts of speech. The syntax chapter examines only those points which cannot be so studied.

Reference numbers in the text relate to chapter number/

paragraph number. Roman numbers refer to the appendices.

The index supplements the references quoted in the chapters and appendices, and should, like them, be fully used in the search for the right structure.

I take this opportunity to express my thanks to Goly Foroughi, Sharare Atabaki Nosratifard and Mahmoud Khanchezzar for their help in checking the examples, to Jeannine and Paul Tys for permission to include their photographs, and to Marilyn Moore for her help in proof-reading. Any remaining shortcomings are my responsibility.

1. Writing

1. General

In other chapters of this book each paragraph is discrete; in other words, as far as possible it does not assume that the student has studied any other paragraphs.

This chapter, on the other hand, is of necessity continuous; that is, each paragraph assumes knowledge of all previous paragraphs in the chapter.

Paragraphs 1/3 to 25 below give the printed forms of the alphabetical letters and other signs. Many forms look different when handwritten; 1/26 and 27 below show handwritten forms.

The writing of the numerals is examined in 9/1.

Chapter 2 shows the pronunciation of the letters and their transcription used in this book.

2. Alphabet and spelling

Persian is written with a modified Arabic alphabet. The general principles of this alphabet are:

- The writing runs from right to left ← .
- There are no capital letters.
- Short vowels (there are three, which we transcribe as *a, o, e*) are mostly not written, but inferred from the outline and context. There is a means of marking these vowels but it is hardly ever seen outside school textbooks.
- Most letters are joined to the letter following them in the same word, i.e. to the left. These are *joined* letters. Almost all of these have a short form when joined to the following letter, and a full form when not so joined.
- A few letters, called *disjoined* letters, are never joined to the following letter. They have only one form.

This book uses the modern reformed spelling. Some older spellings are, however, still encountered, and these are also shown where appropriate.

3 .

| ا *alef* |

The first and commonest letter of the alphabet is called *alef*. It is a *disjoined* letter, never joined to the letter following it. It is pronounced as follows:

- at the beginning of a word, it shows the presence of one of the short vowels *a, o, e* (which are not themselves written)
- in the middle or at the end of a word, it represents the long vowel *ā*.

4 .

| آ *alef madde* |

This variant of ا *alef* is written at the beginning of a word to represent the long vowel *ā*.

5 .

| ب بـ *be* |
| پ پـ *pe* |
| ت تـ *te* |
| ث ثـ *se** |

These four letters called *be, pe, te* and *se* all look alike except for the dot(s) above or below them. They are of course written leftwards ← . They are pronounced respectively *b, p, t* and *s*. They are all joined letters, i.e. joined to the next letter in the word.

Each one has a short form used at the beginning or in the middle of a word, and a full form used at the end of a word or when standing alone.

Combined with ‏ا‎ *alef* or ‏آ‎ *alef madde* (1/3 and 4 above) they appear as follows:

> ‏أب‎ *āb* water (*alef* and *alef madde* are not joined to the next letter, in this case ‏ب‎ *be*)
>
> ‏با‎ *bā* with ⎫ (the letters of the
> ‏پا‎ *pā* foot ⎬ *be* group are joined
> ‏تا‎ *tā* until ⎭ to the *alef* following them)
>
> ‏باب‎ *bāb* chapter (of a book)

* ‏ث‎ *se* occurs only in a very few words, of Arabic origin. The commonest letter for *s* is shown in 1/12 below.

The letters of the ‏ب‎ *be* group are called 'toothed' letters; their short form without its dot(s) is ‏ـ‎, called a 'tooth'. There are other toothed letters, studied below.

6.

> | ‏ن ـن‎ *nun* |
> | --- |

The letter *nun* represents the sound *n*. This is a joined letter, and has two forms: a short form used at the beginning or in the middle of a word, and a full form used at the end of a word or when standing alone. The short form is a tooth (see 1/5 above); the long form is deeper.

> ‏آن‎ *ān* that   ‏نان‎ *nān* bread

7.

> | ‏ی ـی‎ *ye* |
> | --- |

The letter *ye* is a joined letter, with a toothed short form used as are those of the ‏ب‎ *be* group (1/5 above). The long form, used at the end of a word or when the letter stands alone, has no dots. It swoops below the line of print. *ye* has the following pronunciation:

- at the beginning of a word: the consonant *y*
- in the middle of a word: the consonant *y*, or the long vowel *i*, or (less often) the vowel-combination *ei*

- at the end of a word:
    - after a consonant, the long vowel *i*, or (less often) the vowel-combination *ei*; also, at the end of a very few words taken from Arabic, *ā* (an example of which is given in 1/21 below)
    - after a vowel, the syllable *-ye*; very rarely, *i*.

یا	*yā* or	بی	*bi* without
بین	*bein* between	پایان	*pāyān* end
بیابان	*biābān* desert	نایب	*nāyeb* deputy

The combination *āi* is written ...ایی\...ییـ... (آیی beginning a word), the first of the two letters *ye* being silent:

پایین	*pāin* low, down	بیایی	*biāi* you may come
		آیین	*āin* custom

See also 1/8, 21 and 24 below.

In a few words this combination is written with one *ye*: see 1/13.

It is a rule that no vowel other than long *ā* can begin a word in writing. Where a vowel other than *ā* is the first sound, it must be introduced. The commonest letter for introducing a vowel is ا *alef*:

این *in* this

8.

و	*vāv*

The letter *vāv* is a disjoined letter with only one form, extending below the line of print. *vāv* is pronounced:

- at the beginning of a word: *v*
- in the middle or at the end of a word: *v*, or the long vowel *u*, or (less often) the vowel-combination *ou*. At the end of a very few words (all of which are important) it represents the short vowel *o*
- in a few important words it is silent; see 1/13 below.

و *va, o** and   ایوان *eivān* porch

توپ *tup* ball توی *tuye* in

ناو *nāv* warship بو *bu* smell

نو *nou* new تو *to* you

The combination *-ui* is written ...ویی\...ویـ... , the first of the two letters *ye* being silent:

بویی *bui* a smell

See also 1/7, 21 and 24.

The rule given in 1/7 above concerning initial vowels applies here also:

او *u* he, she

The word و pronounced *o* 'and', marked * above, is an exception to this rule.

9.

م ـم مـ *mim*

The letter *mim* is a joined letter. It represents *m*. Its short and full forms are used in the manner described in 1/5 above. The full form has a tail reaching straight down below the line of print.

من *man* I می‌مانیم *mi mānim* we stay

نام *nām* name نیم *nim* half

An initial 'tooth' (see 1/5 above) preceding *mim* is often inverted and raised. Initial *mim* is often also raised when followed by another *mim*:

تمام *tamām* complete می‌نمایم *mi namāyam* I show

نمی‌آییم *nemi āim* we do not come ممنون *mamnun* grateful

10.

د *dāl*
ذ *zāl*

The disjoined letters called *dāl* and *zāl* have only one form each, identical but for the dot. These letters rest on the line of print.

They are sounded respectively *d* and *z*. ذ is not the commonest letter for the sound *z*; that is shown in the next paragraph.

دانایی *dānāi* wisdom   دندان *dandān* tooth

دویدن *davidan* to run   می‌نمایید *mi namāid* you show

می‌داند *mi dānad* he/she knows   آمد *āmad* he/she came

نمودند *namudand* they showed   می‌آید *mi āyad* he/she comes

11.

ر	*re*
ز	*ze*
ژ	*že*

The disjoined letters *re* (sounded *r*), *ze* (sounded *z*) and *že* (sounded *ž*, see 2/3), are identical but for their dots. They each have one form only, which curves down slightly below the line of print.

At first sight this group may seem to be similar to the د *dāl* group. There is in fact no confusion; *re* and *ze* are joined to the previous letter at the head, and they strike immediately downwards, while *dāl* and *zāl* are joined to the previous letter at the angle, and the whole letter remains on the line of writing.

ز *ze* is the commonest letter (out of three possible) used for the sound *z*. The letter ژ *že* and its sound *ž* are very rare.

دارد *dārad* he/she has   در *dar* in, door

دزد *dozd* thief   مرا *marā* me

زیر *zire* beneath   زیبا *zibā* beautiful

                                      آباژور *ābāžur* lampshade

12.

س ـسـ ـس	*sin*
ش ـشـ ـش	*šin*

The letters *sin* and *šin* are joined letters. They represent respectively the sounds *s* and *š* (see 2/3). The short and full forms are used in the same way as those of the *be* group (1/5 above). The short form rests on the line of print, while the flourish of the full form swoops below. س *sin* is by far the commonest letter (out of three possible) for writing the sound *s*.

است *ast* he/she is   پس *pas* then

سی *si* thirty   شام *šām* dinner

پشت *pošt* back   شستن *šostan* to wash

13.

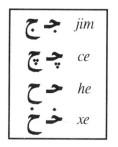

This group of four joined letters is *jim* (sounded *j*), *ce* or *cim* (sounded *c*), *he* (sounded *h*) and *xe* (sounded *x*). See 2/3 for the sounds *c* and *x*. Short and full forms are used as are those of the *be* group, 1/5 above.

ح *he* is the less common of two ways of writing the sound *h*. It is found in words of Arabic origin, and is sometimes called *he hoti* to distinguish it from the commoner letter for *h* given in 1/15 below.

جا *jā* place   خارج *xārej* outside

حاجت *hājat* need   پیچ *pic* screw

چای* *cāi* tea   پایتخت* *pāitaxt* capital city

* *āi* written, exceptionally, with one *ye*; see 1/7 above.

An initial 'tooth' (see 1/5 above) preceding one of these letters is often inverted and raised:

تجارت\تجارت *tejārat* trade

In the syllables خوا *xā*, خود *xod*, خور *xor*, خوش *xoš* and خوی *xi*, the letter و *vāv* is silent:

خواستن *xāstan* to want   خود ، خویش *xod, xiš* oneself

خوردن *xordan* to eat   خوش *xoš* well

9

14.

$$ل\ ل\ \textit{lām}$$

lām is a joined letter, with no dots. It is pronounced *l.* Its full and short forms are used as are those of the *be* group, 1/5 above.

This letter is distinct from ‏ا‎ *alef*, since *alef* is disjoined and *lām* is joined.

‏لباس‎ *lebās* suit (of clothes)   ‏جلو‎ *jelou* ahead
‏خیال‎ *xiāl* imagination   ‏آلمان‎ *ālmān* Germany

The combination *lām + alef* has special forms, one used when it is joined to the previous letter, and another when it is not. The form [‏لا‎] is never used:

‏اسلام‎ *eslām* Islam   ‏لازم‎ *lāzem* necessary

15.

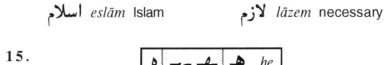

The joined letter called *he* is the commoner of the two letters used for the sound *h.* It is often called *he havvaz* to distinguish it from the less common letter ‏ح‎ given in 1/13 above. ‏ه‎ and its variants all rest on the line, apart from the lower part of the forms ‏ـهـ‎ and ‏ـه‎ . This letter has four forms:

- one used at the beginning of a word or after a disjoined letter: ‏ه‎
- two alternative forms used when the letter is joined on both sides: ‏ـهـ ـهـ‎
- one used at the end of a word or when the letter stands alone: ‏ه‎ .

‏هر‎ *har* every   ‏پاها‎ *pāhā* feet
‏مهمان\مهمان‎ *mehmān* guest   ‏نه‎ *noh* nine
‏راه‎ *rāh* road   ‏تنبیه‎* *tambih* punishment
* the combination ‏نب‎ *[nb]* is pronounced *mb.*

Silent final ‏ه‎ . After the unwritten vowel *e,* the letter ‏ه‎ at the end

10

of a word is silent:

آینده *āyande* future   دیده *dide* seen

خانه *xāne* house   بسته *baste* closed

Silent final ه is also, exceptionally, found after the short unwritten vowel *a* in the expressions

نه *na* no   نه ... نه *na ... na* neither ... nor

When a word ending with silent ه is extended with a suffix, the next letter starts afresh; or, with a few suffixes, the ه is dropped:

خانه *xāne* house   خانه‌ها *xānehā* houses

نامه *nāme* letter   نامه‌ها *nāmehā* letters

میوه *mive* fruit   میوه‌ها\میوجات\میوه‌جات
mivehā/mivejāt fruits

After this silent final ه, any added syllable beginning -*i* is written with its own introductory *alef*:

جمله *jomle* sentence   جمله‌ای *jomlei* a sentence

ریشه *riše* root   ریشه‌ای *rišei* rootlike

Details are given in the discussion of each suffix or other ending as it occurs.

In words such as those shown above the final ه is a graphic device or a grammatical ending. In words with final ه after *e* where the ه is not an ending but part of the root of the word, the ه is sounded *h*. Such words are not numerous:

بده *bedeh* give   متوجه *motavajjeh* attentive

16.

These are the joined letters ک *kāf* (pronounced *k*) and گ *gāf* (pronounced *g*; see also 2/3 for both sounds). They stand on the line of writing; their short and full forms are used in the same way as those of the *be* group (1/5 above). *kāf* has two possible

full forms, ک and ك .

که *ke* that, when   می‌کند *mi konad* he/she does

پزشك\پزشک *pezešk* doctor   مسواك *mesvāk* toothbrush

کار *kār* work   کلم *kalam* cabbage

کلاس *kelās* (school) class   کل *kal* stag

گرم *garm* warm   می‌گوید *mi guyad* he/she says

رنگ *rang* colour   گرگ *gorg* wolf

گاهی *gāhi* sometimes   گل *gol* flower

گلابی *golābi* pear   گمرك *gomrok* customs

17.

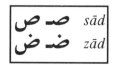

ص ص ص *sād*

ض ض ض *zād*

The letters *sād* and *zād* are joined letters. Their short and full forms are used as are those of the *be* group (1/5 above). The loop rests on the line of print, and the 'flourish' of the full form curves below. These letters represent respectively the sounds *s* and *z*; ص is less common than س *sin* for *s* (1/12 above) and ض is less common than ز *zāl* for *z* (1/11 above). ص and ض mostly occur in words taken from Arabic.

صورت *surat* list   اصل *asl* origin

شخص *šaxs* person   مخصوص *maxsus* special

حاضر *hāzer* present, ready   امضا *emzā* signature

18.

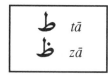

ط *tā*

ظ *zā*

Although the letters ط *tā* and ظ *zā* are joined letters, they have only one form each, which stands on the line of print. They represent respectively the sounds *t* and *z*; ط is less common than ت *te* for *t* (1/5 above) and ظ is less common than ز *zāl* for *z* (1/11 above). ط and ظ mostly occur in words taken from Arabic.

طور *tour* manner, way   شیطان *šeitān* devil

ظهر *zohr* midday   نظامی *nezāmi* military

19.

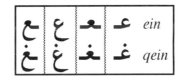

The letters called *ein* and *qein* are joined letters. Each has four forms:

- ـع and ـغ are written at the beginning of a word or after a disjoined letter.
- ـعـ and ـغـ are written when the letter is joined on both sides.
- ع and غ are written at the end of a word after a disjoined letter; or when the letter stands alone.
- ـع and ـغ are written at the end of a word after a joined letter.

You will see that the closed forms are written after a joined letter in the same word, and the open forms when no joined letter precedes in the same word.

At the beginning of a word ع is silent. The formal sound of ع in the middle or at the end of a word is ' (the 'glottal stop'), but it is sometimes dropped; see 2/3.

The sound of غ is *q*, for which see 2/3.

عصر *asr* late afternoon   تعطیل *ta'til* holiday

موضوع *mouzu'* subject   منع *man'* prevention

غایب *qāyeb* absent   تغییر *taqyir* change

دروغ *doruq* lie (untruth)   مبلغ *mablaq* amount

20.

The two joined letters ف *fe* (sounded *f*) and ق *qāf* (sounded *q*, see 2/3) form a group. Their short and full forms are used as are those of the *be* group (1/5 above). All forms lie on the line of print except full-form ق which swoops below.

فكر	*fekr* thought, idea	بيفهم	*bifahm* stupid
برف	*barf* snow	كثيف	*kasif* dirty
آقا	*āqā* gentleman, Mr	انقلاب	*enqelāb* revolution
برق	*barq* lightning, electricity	برقى	*barqi* electric(al)

21. Doubled letters

Two identical consonants with an intervening vowel are written separately:

ممنون mamnun grateful

(short unwritten *a* between the two letters م *m*, long written و *u* between the two letters ن *n*).

Two identical consonants with no intervening vowel are written as one consonant, but pronounced double *when a vowel follows* (see 2/4):

بچه	*bacce* child	نجار	*najjār* carpenter

حتى *hattā* even (see 1/7 above for final ى pronounced *ā*)

1/23 below shows a means of indicating the doubled consonant.

This general rule is broken when two identical consonants come together in the formation of a compound word; 11/2 and 3 explain.

The sound *i* after آ\ا *ā* or و *u* is written with double ى *ye*: ى...\...ييـ.... In this combination the first *ye* is silent and merely functions as a link between the two long vowels:

مى آييم	*mi āim* we come	مى گوييد	*mi guid* you say

See also 1/7 and 8 above, and 1/24 below.

In a few words the combination *āi* is written with one *ye*: see 1/13.

22. Whole alphabet

Here is the alphabet in its Persian order; see 2/3 for details of pronunciation. For the sounds *t, s, h* and *z* the alternative letters are graded in order of frequency. 1 indicates the most common; letters graded 2 to 4 are mostly found in words taken from Arabic. The two letters pronounced *q* are of roughly equal frequency; ق is found mainly in words taken from Arabic.

Letter	Name	Sound; frequency *t, s, h, z, q*	Reference
(*آ	*alef madde*	Initial: ā)	1/4
ا	*alef*	Initial: shows *a, o, e* or introduces *u, i, ou, ei*. Middle or final: *ā*.	1/3
ب	*be*	*b*	1/5
پ	*pe*	*p*	
ت	*te*	*t* 1	
ث	*se*	*s* 3	
ج	*jim*	*j*	1/13
چ	*ce*	*c*	
ح	*he (hoti)*	*h* 2	
خ	*xe*	*x*	
د	*dāl*	*d*	1/10
ذ	*zāl*	*z* 4	
ر	*re*	*r*	1/11
ز	*ze*	*z* 1	
ژ	*že*	*ž*	
س	*sin*	*s* 1	1/12
ش	*šin*	*š*	
ص	*sād*	*s* 2	1/17
ض	*zād*	*z* 2	
ط	*tā*	*t* 2	1/18
ظ	*zā*	*z* 3	
ع	*ein*	Initial: silent. Middle or final: '	1/19
غ	*qein*	*q*	

ف	*fe*	*f*	1/20
ق	*qāf*	*q*	
ك	*kāf*	*k*	1/16
گ	*gāf*	*g*	
ل	*lām*	*l*	1/14
م	*mim*	*m*	1/9
ن	*nun*	*n*	1/6
و	*vāv*	Initial: *v*. Middle or final: *v, u, ou, (o)*	1/8
		After خ : often silent	1/13
ه	*he (havvaz)*	*h*; but when final after *e (a)*: silent	1/15
ی	*ye*	Initial: *y*. Middle: *y, i. ei*. Final: *i, ei, ye*	1/7
		ییـ\یی after و\ا : *i* (first *ye* silent)	1/7, 8
		(Final in a few words from Arabic: *ā*)	1/7

* آ *alef madde* is only a variant of ا *alef* which is the first letter. But in many dictionaries all words beginning آ are listed before words beginning ا .

The word اردو *ordu* 'camp' helps to recall the four disjoined letters or families of letters.

23. Non-alphabetical signs

Certain non-alphabetical signs, most of them rarely used, exist to fix the pronunciation of the word. The main ones are:

- vowels ˙˙˙ *a* (called *fathe* or *zebar*), ˙˙˙ *o* (*zamme* or *piš*), ... *e* (*kasre* or *zir*), after ا at the beginning of a word, or after a consonant in any position:

$$آن اَسب بُزُرگ ان asbe bozorg that big horse$$

- vowel-combinations ˆو˙˙˙ *ou* and ˆی˙˙˙ *ei*, after ا at the beginning of a word, or after a consonant in any position:

$$نَو nou new \qquad ایوان eivān porch$$

- two marks peculiar to consonants:

  - ˙˙˙ called *tašdid*, written above a consonant to show that

16

it is pronounced double:

بچّه *bacce* child

- ْ ... called *sokun* or *jazm*, written above a consonant to show that it has no vowel after it:

اَسْب *asb* horse

The signs shown above are rarely encountered outside schoolbooks. One sign which, however, is almost always shown is the adverbial ending called *tanvin* and written اً... pronounced *-an* (short *a*) after a consonant:

مرتبًا *morattaban* regularly   تقریبًا *taqriban* approximately

معمولاً *ma'mulan* usually   تلفنًا *telefonan* by telephone

حقیقت *haqiqat* truth   حقیقتًا *haqiqatan* truly, in truth

When this ending is added to a word taken from Arabic and ending in *e* + silent ه (see 1/15 above), both these are dropped and replaced by تًا... *-atan*:

قاعده *qā'ede* rule   قاعدتًا *qā'edatan* as a rule

We also still encounter in some dictionaries and older texts the original Arabic spelling ة.... . The pronunciation is the same, *-atan*:

(حقیقةً) for حقیقتًا *haqiqatan*   (قاعدةً) for قاعدتًا *qā'edatan*

See 7/2 for more about the endings اً... *-an* and تًا... *-atan*.

24. | ء *hamze* |

ء , called *hamze*, is a letter not listed in the alphabet. It is never joined to anything. It never stands at the beginning of a word. Its basic form is as shown here, but it appears and sounds differently according to whether it is used in Persian words, or in words taken from Arabic.

***hamze* in Persian words.** In Persian words *hamze* may be written over silent final ه (1/15 above), to represent *ye* (the *ezāfe*, see Appendix II):

17

خانهٔ ایشان *xāneye išān* his/her/their house

میوهٔ تازه *miveye tāze* fresh fruit

The *hamze* representing *ye* (the *ezāfe*) is usually written only when extra clarity is wanted; otherwise it is often left unwritten:

خانه ایشان *xāneye išān*

میوه تازه *miveye tāze*

We also encounter the form ئ (now little used) for -*iye*, showing the *ezāfe* after words ending in ی *i*:

صندلی راحتی *(for* صندلئ راحتی*)* *sandaliye rāhati* easy chair

In older Persian, including some dictionaries, we find the combination ئی\ئـ instead of یی\یـ (1/7, 8, 21 above), for *i* after *ā* or *u*:

شیمیایی (earlier شیمیائی) *šimiāi* chemical

بگویید (earlier بگوئید) *beguid* say

and ةٔ... instead of modern ای...ه *-ei/-e i* at the end of a word (1/15 above):

جملهای (earlier جملةٔ) *jomlei* a sentence

قهوهای رنگ (earlier قهوةٔ رنگ) *qahvei rang* brown

خستهای (earlier خستةٔ) *xaste i* you are tired

In a few words taken from other languages the form ژ is used to mark the transition from one vowel to another:

ژوئن *žuan* June (from French juin)

گازوئیل *gāzuil* fuel oil, diesel ایدئولوژیست *ideoložist* ideologist

hamze in words taken from Arabic. In words taken from Arabic, *hamze* may occur before or after any letter in the middle or at the end of a word:

- in the middle, أ *a'/'a,* ؤ *o',* ئو *'u,* ئـ *':*

متأسف *mota'assef* sorry   تأسیس *ta'sis* foundation

مؤمن *mo'men* believer   مسئول *mas'ul* responsible

مسأله\مسئله *mas'ale/masale* problem

Middle أ is often written ا:

18

متاسف *mota'assef,* مساله *masale.*

- at the end, it is normally written by itself, and is usually silent in Persian:

جزء *joz* part

Some words written with final ا... -*ā* can still be found with their original Arabic spelling ء ا... . The pronunciation is the same, as the ء is silent:

ابتدا *ebtedā* beginning (formerly ابتدا ء)

ء *hamze* must not be confused with short-form ـع (1/19 above) which it visibly resembles.

25. نستعلیق *nasta'liq* script

The form of script shown in 1/3-24 above is called نسخ *nasx.* It is the script used in newspapers, notices and mass-circulated books. An older calligraphic script form, called نستعلیق *nasta'liq,* is often used for fine printing, titles and posters. In *nasx* the line of print is more or less level, whereas in *nasta'liq* each group of letters tends to 'cascade' above its predecessor, so: ـیـ. This and other important differences in style are summarised below:

	nasx		*nasta'liq*

Standard forms:

'cascading'	فارسی *fārsi* Persian	فارسی
	دوستان من *dustāne man* my friends	دوستان من
خ ح ج	خجالت *xejālat* shame	خجالت
	پیچ *pic* screw	پیچ
ك گ	کوچك *kucek* small	کوچک
	گرگ *gorg* wolf	گرگ
کا گا	کارگر *kārgar* workman	کارگر

بنگاه *bongāh* institution   بنگاه

کل گل   کلید *kelid* key   کلید

گل *gol* flower   گل

لا ـلا   بالا *bālā* above   بالا

کلاس *kelās* class   کلاس

tooth or ف ـ\ق\   بی *bi* without   بی

ک\گ\ل   کافی *kāfi* sufficient   کافی

+ final ـی   ترکی *torki* Turkish   ترکی

ملی *melli* national   ملی

Optional alternative forms:

س ش   نشستن *nešastan* to sit   نشستن

شش *šeš* six   شش

initial ها   پسرها *pesarhā* sons   پسرها

initial ـه   هر *har* every   هر

کوتاهتر *kutāhtar* shorter   کوتاهتر

final joined ـه   لوله *lule* tube   لوله

بیمه *bime* insurance   بیمه

final ـی after any   دوستی *dusti* friendship   دوستی

joined letter   عراقی *erāqi* Iraqi   عراقی

Here, for comparison, is a poem by عمر خیّام *omare xayyām* Omar Khayyam, in *nasx* and in *nasta'liq*, with two translations, one close, and one free by Edward Fitzgerald:

خیّام اگر ز باده مستی خوش باش
با لاله رخی ومی نشستی خوش باش
چون عاقبت کار جهان نیستی است
انگار که نیستی ، چو هستی خوش باش
عمر جیّام

خیّام اگر ز باده مستی خوش باش
بالاله رخی و می نشستے خوش باش
چون عاقبت کار جهان نیستی است
انگار که نیستی چو هستی خوش باش
عمر خیّام

xayyām, agar z bāda* mast i, xoš bāš;

bā lāleroxi o mi nešasti, xoš bāš.

cun āqabate kāre jahān nisti st,

engār ke nisti; co hasti, xoš bāš

omare xayyām

(* **ز باده** *z bāda* = **از شراب** *az šarāb* 'from wine')

Khayyam, if thou art drunk with wine, be glad!

If seated next one with tulip cheeks, be glad!

Since the world's work has no hereafter, think then

Thou mightst not be - but since thou art, be glad!

And if the Wine you drink, the Lip you press,

End in the Nothing all Things end in - yes,

Then fancy while Thou art, Thou art but what

Thou shalt be - Nothing - Thou shalt not be less.

transl. Edward Fitzgerald

26. Standard handwritten forms

The most important features of standard handwriting are shown below. Many of them reflect the نستعلیق *nasta'liq* script shown in 1/25 above.

ا *alef*. When not joined to a previous letter, ا *alef* is written downwards. Following a joined letter, it is written upwards:

ارزان ۱ رزان *arzān* cheap   با با *bā* with

See below for the writing of *alef* after ل *lām* and after ك *kāf*.

Dots. Two dots are written like a hyphen - ; three dots form a rough ring written in either direction as convenient, ؇ or ؇ :

توپ توپ *tup* ball   چراغ حراغ *cerāq* lamp

ج etc. Letters of the ج *jim* group are often joined to the preceding letter at the upper right corner in print, but always at the upper left corner (i.e. at the beginning of the outline) in handwriting. A preceding initial tooth is almost always inverted (see 1/13 above). Compare the forms:

نخ نخ *nax* thread   خجالت خجالت *xejālat* shame

م *mim*. After a joined letter, م *mim* should be approached from the top, and the 'bead' written anticlockwise ؇. A preceding initial tooth is almost always inverted (see 1/9 above):

دلم د لم *delam* my heart نمودن نمودن *namudan* to show

This handwritten form effectively distinguishes middle joined ـم *mim* from middle joined ـع *ein*, which is always approached from below and written clockwise ؇ :

معروف معروف *ma'ruf* well known

Middle tooth. See 1/5. A middle tooth, i.e. one joined on both sides, has a special raised handwritten form before م *mim* or ر/ز *re/ze*. Examine the forms:

رفتم رفتم *raftam* I went   میز میز *miz* table

ليتر ليتَر *litr* litre

Initial and middle ـص *sād* and ـض *zād* have a tooth after their loop; this tooth must not be omitted in handwriting. It behaves like a middle tooth before م *mim* or ز\ر *re/ze*:

صمیمی صمیمی *samimi* sincere مصر مصر *mesr* Egypt

ط *tā* and ظ *zā*. Unlike ـص *sād* and ـض *zād* (see immediately above), ط *tā* and ظ *zā* have no tooth after the loop. The loop is written first, then the upright:

چطور چطور *cetour* how نظامی نظامی *nezāmi* military

س *sin* and ش *šin*. In all but the most careful handwriting, the indentations of these letters are flattened out into a smooth curve, thus:

دوست دوست *dust* friend شب شب *šab* evening

پیش پیش *piš* before بیشتر بیشتر *bištar* more

لا\لا *lām-alef*. See 1/14 above. In writing this combination, detach the *alef* and write it downwards, either vertically towards the foot of the *lām* or at an angle to its middle. Compare printed and handwritten forms:

لا لا لا لا لا لا لا *lā*

سلام سلام *salām* hello لازم لازم *lāzem* necessary

ک *kāf* and گ *gāf*. Examine the handwritten forms shown below. The downstroke is written vertically ل , the headstroke(s) ◞ last. In the forms with *alef* and/or *lām*, the circle is written anticlockwise ک کـ, approaching from below if the combination is joined to the preceding letter, so: کـ.

گ گ ک ک گ گ ك ک ک ک *k, g*

گا گا گا گا گا گا گا گا *kā, gā*

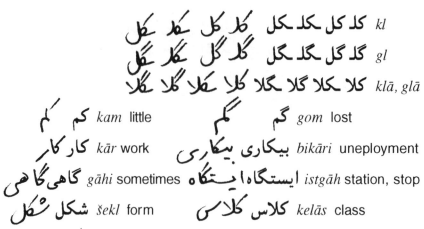

The form ك is not used in handwriting.

ه *he*. The middle form ـهـ is seldom used in handwriting; the simpler form ـٯـ is written instead. The final form joined to the preceding letter, printed ـه, is very often simplified in handwriting to ـه:

چهار\چهار چهار *cahār* four

رفته رفته *rafte* gone   سه *se* three

Final ى *ye*. When final ى *ye* is preceded by a tooth, or by any of the letters ف\ق *fe/qāf*, ک\گ *kāf/gāf* or ل *lām*, the junction is handwritten as a sharp angle, and the *ye* loses its first curve:

جایی جایی *jāi* a place   دوستی دوستی *dusti* friendship

برقی برقی *barqi* electric(al)   کی کی *ki* who

فصلی فصلی *fasli* seasonal

But after other joined letters (including ص\ض with its tooth, see above) the junction is rounded, and *ye* has both its curves:

کمی کمی *kami* a little   راضی راضی *rāzi* satisfied

27. شکسته *šekaste* handwriting

Many Iranians use so-called *šekaste* or 'broken' handwriting, a form greatly simplified for the writer but often very difficult for the inexperienced reader. *šekaste* also draws some of its forms from *nasta'liq*, shown in 1/25 above. The forms shown below are used in addition to the simplifications found in standard handwriting (1/26).

Dots. In the 'toughest' *šekaste* many dots may be left out altogether. Or they may stray away from the outline to which they belong; occasionally one and two dots on successive letters may be grouped as three (i.e. in a ring):

تنها شها *tanhā* alone

(Dis)joined letters. Often, the letters و ژ ز ز ر ذ د ا, in principle not joined to the following letter, are nevertheless so joined in *šekaste*. Common combinations:

اد	باد	*bād* wind
ال	خیال	*xiāl* imagination
دم	شدم	*šodam* I became
دو	دور	*dur* far
ده	دیده	*dide* seen
را	رادیو	*rādio* radio
رد	دارد	*dārad* he/she/it has
زی	زیاد	*ziād* much
وا	مواد	*mavādd* materials
ود	بود	*bud* he/she/it was
ول	پول	*pul* money

ه *he.* Two *nasta'liq* forms for this letter are used in *šekaste*; the final form joined to a previous letter, and the detached syllable **ها** *hā*:

بچه ها بچه ها *baccehā* children

Modified final letters. Some letters, the most common being ن ت and ى, have modified final forms in *šekaste*:

ـس ت ـس است ا *ast* is   توت تو *tut* mulberry

نْ ن نان نان *nān* bread   من من *man* I

ى بر بری برای *barāye* for   ایرانی ایرانی *irāni* Iranian

28. Persian transcription

The transcription of foreign words (mostly names) often reflects the fact that French was once the most widely taught European language in Iran. Whatever the source language, short and long vowels are often not distinguished. Examples:

یونسکو *yunesko* UNESCO   پاریس *pāris* Paris

واشنگتن *vāšengton* Washington   لندن *landan* London

ژنو *ženev* Geneva   نیویورك *nyuyork* New York

فاكس *faks* fax   ژاپن *žāpon* Japan

مكانیزه *mekanize* mechanised   گازوئیل *gāzuil* gasoil, diesel

اتریش *otriš* Austria   ایتالیا *itālyā* Italy

آتاترك *ātātork* Atatürk   مسكو *moskou* Moscow

Since no Persian word can begin with two consonants having no intervening vowel, any such foreign word has to be adapted. Initial s + consonant becomes ..اسـ *es-*; any other initial group acquires an intervening vowel:

اسكتلند *eskotland* Scotland   فرانسه *ferānse* France

نیویورك *nyuyork* 'New York' is an exception to this rule, probably because its second letter ـى *y* is a semi-vowel.

26

2. Pronunciation

1. Transcription

See 1/22-24 for the transcription used in this book for Persian writing.

2. Long and short vowels; diphthongs (vowel-combinations)

It is important to distinguish between the three short vowels and their long counterparts, and between these and the two vowel-combinations. Pronounce as follows:

Short: *a*   as a in Southern English 'bat'   من *man* I

     e   between e and i in English 'bet' and 'bit';   دل *del* heart
        ending a word: like French é in 'café'   سه *se* three

     o   between o and u in English 'pot' and 'put'   تند *tond* fast

Long: *ā*   between the a's in English 'dark' and 'talk';
        ā is the deep sound which you produce
        when the doctor tells you to say 'a-a-ah'.   آن *ān* that

     i   as i in English 'machine'   نیم *nim* half

     u   as u in English 'rule' or in German 'Buch'   طول *tul* length

Combinations: *ei*   as ei in English 'weight'   میل *meil* inclination

            ou   as ou in English 'soul'   نو *nou* new

3. Consonants

The consonants transcribed *b, p, t, s, j, d, z, f, m, n, v* are pronounced much as in English. The other consonants merit closer attention. Some easier ones first:

     c   as ch in English 'rich'   پیچ *pic* screw

     h   as h in English 'how'. It is pronounced   حال *hāl* conditon
        wherever transcribed *h*, even in the   پهن *pahn* broad
        middle or at the end of the word.   ده *dah* ten

     x   as ch in Scots 'loch', Welsh 'bach' or
        German 'Buch'; or j in Spanish 'bajo'   خون *xun* blood

     r   rolled r, as in Italian or Spanish. It is   روز *ruz* day

27

always pronounced wherever it occurs, دور *dur* far
never dropped as in some English درس *dars* lesson
speech.

ž as j in French 'jour', or s in English 'treasure' ویژه *viže* special

š as <u>sh</u> in English 'she' شام *šām* dinner

l always 'light' as in English 'leaf', never
'dark' as in English 'wall' لال *lāl* dumb

y always a consonant, as <u>y</u> in English 'year',
never with a vowel sound as in English 'my' یا *yā* or

' : ء and ع. The transcription **'** represents the 'glottal stop', i.e. a catch in the breath. It is the sound heard in some speech of Southeastern England, or parts of Scotland: "wo' a lo' o' " for "what a lot of". The stop is spelt sometimes with ء *(hamze)*, sometimes with ع. In modern Persian it is pronounced only in the middle or at the end of words taken from Arabic, and not always then. It is a very weak sound, barely audible in the speech of most Iranians:

- *in the middle of a word*, when spelt with ع the stop is usually pronounced:

  ساعت *sā'at* hour, clock   جمعه *jom'e* Friday

  When spelt with ء it is either pronounced weakly, or not at all. The Arabic spellings for *hamze* أ , ؤ and ئـ are found, often with alternatives:

  متأسف\متاسف *mota'assef/motaassef* sorry
  مسئله\مسأله\مساله *mas'ale/masale* problem
  سؤال\سئوال *so'āl/soāl* question
  مسئولیت *mas'uliyat/masuliyat* responsibility

- *at the end of a word*, ء or ع after a consonant is usually silent, though some people pronounce the ع as a stop:

  جزء *joz* part   ربع *rob/rob'* quarter

  but when an *ezāfe* (Appendix II) is added to such a word, the ء or ع ceases to be final and is usually pronounced:

  جزء این مبلغ *joz'e in mablaq* part of this amount

ربع قرض *rob'e qarz* a quarter of the loan

Final ء after a vowel is found mostly in older spellings, and is silent; final ع after a vowel is usually pronounced as a stop:

استثنا *estesnā* exception (formerly استثناء)

نوع *nou'* kind, sort

No word begins with ء *hamze* . ع at the beginning of a word is silent:

عضو *ozv* member   عادت *ādat* custom

q. This sound is the 'voiced' or hard equivalent of *x*, shown above; its nearest European equivalent is French <u>r</u> in 'Marie' or German <u>r</u> in 'fahren'. This sound is the everyday pronunciation of both غ and ق:

آقا *āqā* gentleman, Mr   مبلغ *mablaq* amount

Some people retain for some words the original Arabic pronunciation of ق which is that of *k* pronounced very deep in the throat. Since this happens in only a few words, and many Persians confuse the two sounds anyway in their attempt to differentiate, we will show the pronunciation *q* throughout, which is always correct for both letters.

k. *k* has two sounds:

- before *ā, o, u, ou* or a consonant it sounds like <u>c</u> or <u>k</u> in English 'cook':

كار *kār* work   می کنم *mi konam* I do

كوچكتر *kucektar* smaller

- anywhere else, it sounds like *k* but is 'palatalised', i.e. there is a slight *y*-sound after it; we can imagine its being represented as k^y:

كم *kam* [k^y*am*] a little   يك *yek* [*yek*^{y}] one

If you know Russian, imagine pronouncing a (hypothetical) soft 'кь'. This is similar to palatalised Persian *k*.

29

g. *g* has two sounds:

- before *ā, o, u, ou* or a consonant it sounds like hard **g** in English 'good':

گم *gom* lost   می‌گویم *mi guyam* I say

بزرگتر *bozorgtar* bigger

- anywhere else, it sounds like *g* but is palatalised in the same way as is *k*:

گرفت *gereft [g^yereft]* he took   سگ *sag [sag^y]* dog

بزرگ *bozorg [bozorg^y]* big

If you know Russian, imagine pronouncing a soft 'гь'.

At no time is *g* pronounced like soft **g** in English 'gem'.

Because palatalisation follows a simple rule with no exceptions, it will not be shown in the transcription.

mb: ـنب . The combination ـنب *[nb]* is pronounced *mb*:

شنبه *šambe* Saturday

4 . Doubled letters

Doubled consonants (i. e. two identical consonants with no intervening vowel, see 1/21 and 23) are pronounced double, that is, held for longer than single consonants, when followed by a vowel in the same word or phrase:

بچه *bacce* child (pronounced as if transcribed *bac-ce*)

We sound doubled consonants in this manner in a few English words, for example 'midday', pronounced as if spelt *mid-day*.

A doubled consonant not followed by a vowel in the same word or phrase is pronounced single:

مهم است *mohemm ast* it is important

but: مهمتر *mohemtar* (for *[mohemmtar]*) more important

حقاً *haqqan* rightfully

but: حق شناس *haq šenās* (for *[haqq šenās]*) grateful

The spellings ـﯾﯽ\ﺍﯾﯽ and ـﯾﯽ\آﯾﯽ are pronounced *āi*; the spelling ـﯾﯽ\ﻭﯾﯽ is pronounced *ui* or (in one or two words) *oi*:

بالايی *bālāi* upper   می آيد *mi āid* you come

راستگويی *rāstgui* truthfulness   دويی *doi* duality

Avoid the wrong pronunciation *[yi]* for this doubled letter; the first *ye* does no more than mark the transition, and is silent. See 1/7, 8 and 24.

5 . Stress

In any word of more than one syllable, we stress one of the syllables, i.e. pronounce it more strongly than the rest. The position of the stress is regular in Persian. In this paragraph, and at certain other points in the book, we mark the vowel of the stressed syllable with an accent ..´:

Verbs. See 5/1 for the definition of a verb. Verbs and their derivatives are stressed as follows:

- When the verb or verbal derivative has no prefix, it is stressed on the last syllable, discounting any personal ending. Compare

  نوشتن *nevštán* to write   نويسنده *nevisandé* writer

  نوشت *nevéšt* he/she wrote   نوشته *nevešté* written

  with

  دارم *dáram* I have   گرفتند *geréftand* they took

  باشد *bášad* let it be   هستيم *hástim* we are

  The one exception to this rule is that the auxiliary verb of the future tense (5/27) is stressed on the personal ending when the verb is affirmative:

  خواهم رفت *xāhám raft* I shall go

- when the verb or verbal derivative has one prefix or more, the first or only prefix (even when written separately) takes the stress:

ننوشتم *nánevestam* I didn't write

ندارم *nádāram* I have not

می نویسم *mí nevisam* I write

نمی نویسم *némi nevisam* I don't write

بیایید! *bíāid!* Come!   نباشد *nábāšad* let it not be

ننوشته *náneveste* not written/unwritten

- in the future tense, the auxiliary verb takes the stress of the whole tense, following the rules given in the preceding two indents:

خواهم نوشت *xāhám nevešt* I shall write

نخواهم نوشت *náxāham nevešt* I shall not write

- in compound verbs (5/29), the stress of the whole verb falls on the non-verbal element in the affirmative and on the negative prefix in the negative:

کار می کردم *kā́r mi kardam* I was working

کار نمی کردم *kār némi kardam* I was not working

Interjections and conjunctions. Interjections, and many conjunctions, are stressed on the first syllable:

بله *bále* yes   نخیر *náxeir* no

اگر *ágar* if   ولی *váli* but

چرا *cérā* why

Other words. Words other than verbs, interjections or conjunctions are stressed on the last syllable of the root (i.e. the word without any additions):

کتاب *ketā́b* book   رنگزن *rangzán* painter

بیرون *birún* outside   شما *šomā́* you

قشنگ *qašáng* beautiful   دوازده *davāzdáh* twelve

Suffixes. The stress rules for suffixes (syllables added to words, including any written detached), and for personal endings of verbs are:

32

- The following are unstressed and have no effect on stress:
  - personal endings of verbs *(-am, -i, -ad, -im, -id, -and)*, however written, other than those of the future auxiliary in the affirmative (see above)
  - the *ezāfe -e* and *-ye* (Appendix II), however written
  - the indefinite suffix *-i* and the relative suffix *-i* (Appendix III), however written
  - the direct-object suffix را *rā* (Appendix IV)
  - the possessive and pronoun-object suffixes م... *-am*, ت... *-et/at*, ش... *-eš/aš* etc. (3/11, 4/3).

- All others assume the stress of the word to which they relate, even if written separately. The main stressed suffixes are:
  - all plural suffixes: ها *-hā́*, ان... *-ā́n*, گان... *-egā́n*, ات... *-ā́t*, جات... *-(e)jā́t*, ین... *-ín*, ون... *-ún* (3/4)
  - the adjective suffixes تر... *-tár*, ترین... *-tarín* (3/9, 10), ه... *-é* (9/6), ی...\ای... *-í*, گی... *-egí* (11/3), and the abstract noun suffixes ی... *-í*, گی... *-egí* (11/2), together with other less common noun and adjective suffixes explained in 11/2 and 11/3.
  - the ordinal-number suffixes م... *-óm*, مین... *-omín* (9/3).

In English, the vowel of an unstressed syllable often loses its typical sound and becomes neutral; examples are the a in 'asleep' and the o's in 'production'. In Persian, all the vowels of a word, including those in unstressed syllables, keep their typical sound. The neutral sound of a in English 'asleep' does not exist in Persian:

بزرگترین *bozorgtarín* biggest

پنجره‌ها *panjarehā́* windows

Vocative stress of the noun. See 3/1 for the definition of a noun. The rule for stress given under 'other words' above applies to nouns when the noun is *spoken about*. If we address a person, the noun denoting that person is then stressed on its *first* syllable. This is called 'vocative' stress. Compare:

این آقا پیر است. *in āqā́ pir ast.* This gentleman is old.

خانم نیست. *xānóm nist.* Madame isn't (in).

بچه ها می خوابند. *baccehā́ mi xāband.*
The children are sleeping.

with: ببخشید آقا. *bebaxšid ā́qā.* Excuse me, sir.

بفرمایید خانم. *befarmāid xā́nom.* Here you are, ma'am.

خانمها و آقایان *xā́nomhā va ā́qāyān* Ladies and gentlemen

بچه ها ، وقت خواب شده. *báccehā, vaqte xāb šode.*
Children, it's ('become') bedtime.

6. Colloquial pronunciation

The Persian of this book is that of educated speech. But all Persian speakers, whatever their education, use what we can call 'standard' pronunciation in more formal contexts, and 'colloquial' pronunciation for everyday speech. A simple parallel can be drawn in English speech: standard would be 'he is not', colloquial 'he isn't'. Each is correct, depending on the occasion. Persian colloquial pronunciation is shown between angular quotation marks ‹...› in this book. The main elements of colloquial pronunciation are:

- The syllable *ān* becomes ‹un› or ‹on› in almost all words; the syllable *ām* becomes ‹um› or ‹om› in a few words:

  آن *ān* ‹un, on› that   آمد *āmad* ‹umad, omad›
  he/she came

- The direct-object suffix را *rā* becomes ‹ro› after a vowel, ‹o› or ‹ro› after a consonant:

  او را *u rā* ‹u ro› him/her   آن را *ān rā* ‹on o, on ro› it

- Many irregular present stems of verbs have a colloquial form, shorter than the standard form:

34

دادن *dādan* to give, present stem ... ده *deh-* ‹d-›:

می‌دهم *mi deham* ‹mi dam› I give

بدهیم *bedehim* ‹bedim› let's give

- The 3rd-person singular ending د... *-ad* of the present tense becomes ‹-e› after a consonant; the 2nd- and 3rd-person plural endings ید... *-id* and ند... *-and* of all tenses and the imperative become ‹-in› and ‹-an› respectively:

می‌ماند *mi mānad* ‹mi mune› he/she stays

نمی‌دانید *nemi dānid* ‹nemi dunin› you don't know

رفتند *raftand* ‹raftan› they went

- است *ast* 'is' becomes ‹-e› after a word ending in a consonant:

اینطور است *intour ast* ‹intour e› it is/it's so

- The dropping of the glottal stop (2/3 above) is even more widespread in colloquial pronunciation, some people dropping the stop altogether:

ساعت *sā'at* ‹sāat› hour, clock, watch

متأسفم. *mota'assefam* ‹motaassefam›. I'm sorry.

- The *ezāfe* (3/5, 8; Appendix II) is often omitted:

توی خانهٔ علی *tuye xāneye ali* ‹tu xāne ali› in Ali's house

راه آهن *rāhe āhan* ‹rāh āhan› railway

- A few words have their own colloquial form. Common ones are:

خوب *xub* ‹xob› good

دیگر *digar* ‹dige› other

Colloquial pronunciation is represented in Persian writing only in cartoon captions, dialogue, comic strips, popular advertisements and the like.

The applications of colloquial pronunciation are given in detail where they arise throughout this book.

7 . Arabic forms

Most Arabic words and expressions incorporated into Persian are pronounced in a Persian manner. These forms are examined in Chapter 10.

تخت جمشید *taxte jamšid* Persepolis

3. Nouns and Adjectives

1. Nouns - general

A noun is a word denoting a person, creature, place, thing or idea. The nouns shown in this chapter are mostly simple nouns, i.e. not derived from other parts of speech.

Simple nouns are usually stressed on the last syllable (see 2/5):

کتاب *ketāb* book

نامه *nāmé* letter

See 5/20 and 11/2 for the derivation of nouns from other parts of speech, and for compound nouns.

2. Definite and indefinite nouns

A noun is definite when its identity is known, and indefinite when its identity is not known. Persian has no definite article corresponding to English 'the'. A Persian noun in its basic form is either definite or indefinite, depending on the context:

شخص *šaxs* (the) person   خیابان *xiābān* (the) street

ماه *māh* (the) month   کلاه *kolāh* (the) hat

جا *jā* (the) place   پارو *pāru* (the) spade

خانه *xāne* (the) house   کشتی *kašti* (the) ship

To make the noun clearly indefinite ('a, an ...' etc.), the suffix -*i* can be added. This indefinite suffix does not affect the stress of the word:

*   After a consonant, the suffix is spelt ی... :

    شخصی *šaxsi* a person, some person

    خیابانی *xiābāni* a street

    ماهی *māhi* a month, any month

    کلاهی *kolāhi* a hat

*   After a vowel ا *ā* or و *u*, it is written یی... :

    جایی *jāi* a place

    پارویی *pārui* a spade

37

Do not pronounce this combination یی as *[-yi]*; the first letter *ye* is silent.

- After a silent final ه (see 1/15), it is written with a separate ای:

  خانه‌ای *xānei* a house, any house

- For a noun ending in ی... *-i* in the basic form, the indefinite form is the same:

  کشتی *kašti* ship, the ship, a ship

  صندلی *sandali* chair, the chair, a chair

When a series of nouns connected with و *va/o* 'and' is made indefinite, only the last noun carries the indefinite suffix:

کاغذ و مدادی *kāqaz o medādi* a paper and pencil

پسر و دختری *pesar o doxtari* a son and (a) daughter
  or: a boy and a girl

but in an indefinite series connected with یا *yā* 'or', the indefinite suffix is normally repeated:

ساعتی یا روزی *sā'ati yā ruzi* an hour or a day

مدادی یا قلمی *medādi yā qalami* a pencil or (a) pen

The uses of the suffix ی... *-i* are summarised in Appendix III.

See also 3/3 below.

Countable and uncountable. The indefinite suffix is added mostly to indefinite nouns which are *countable*, i.e. denoting persons, things etc. which can exist in separate units. It is rarely attached to *uncountable* nouns, which denote things, ideas etc. found only in a mass. Compare:

آیا قلمی هست؟ *āyā qalami hast?* Is there a pen?
  (countable, indefinite suffix)

with   آیا نان هست؟ *āyā nān hast?* Is there any bread?
  (uncountable, no suffix)

Some Persian nouns can be used either as countable or uncountable, depending on their meaning. One such is جا *jā*:

38

جا هست. *jā hast.* There is space/room. (uncountable)

جایی هست. *jāi hast.* There is a place (= vacancy, seat,
countable).

The indefinite suffix is not used in the middle of an *ezāfe*
construction (see 3/5 and 8 below).

3. Definite direct-object suffix را *rā*

When a definite noun is the direct object of a verb (see 5/6), the
definite direct-object suffix را *rā* is added to the noun. This suffix
is written detached from its noun. The suffix does not affect the
stress of the noun:

كتاب را گرفت. *ketāb rā gereft.* He/She took the book.

نامه را نوشته اند. *nāme rā nevešte and.*
They have written the letter.

To make the noun in these sentences indefinite, we need only
remove the definite direct-object suffix را :

كتاب گرفت. *ketāb gereft.* He/She took a book.

نامه نوشته اند. *nāme nevešte and.* They have written a letter.

which sentences are correct as they stand. If we then add the
indefinite suffix (3/2 above)

كتابی گرفت. *ketābi gereft.*

نامه ای نوشته اند. *nāmei nevešte and.*

we get a stronger indefinite meaning, 'He/She took some book or
other', 'They have written some letter'.

When a series of direct-object nouns is connected with و *va/o* 'and',
the direct-object suffix را is added only after the last noun:

كاغذ و مداد را گرفت. *kāqaz va medād rā gereft.*
He took the paper and pencil.

پسر و دختر را دیدند. *pesar o doxtar rā didand.*
They saw the boy and girl.

The indefinite suffix ی... *-i* and the definite direct-object suffix
may be used together, giving the meaning or implied meaning of the

English 'a certain ...'. Compare

می‌خواهند خانه بخرند. *mi xāhand xāne bexarand*
> They want to buy a house (as yet unknown).

and می‌خواهند خانه را بخرند. *mi xāhand xāne rā bexarand*
> They want to buy the house (one known to all).

with می‌خواهند خانه‌ای را بخرند. *mi xāhand xānei rā bexarand*
> They want to buy a (certain) house (one known to them).

See 3/13 below for a similar structure having indefinite *-i* and definite direct-object را *rā* together.

In older Persian we also find the suffix را *rā* showing an *in*direct object, i.e. with the meaning of the English 'to'. This survives today only in some set expressions, the commonest of which is probably

خدا را شکر *xodā rā šokr* Thank God ('Thanks to God')

Colloquial pronunciation. See 2/6. The direct-object suffix را is pronounced colloquially ‹ro› or ‹o› after a consonant, ‹ro› after a vowel:

استاد را ندیدم. ‹ostād ro/ostād o› nadidam.
> I didn't see the professor.

The uses of the suffix را *rā* are summarised in Appendix IV.

4 . Plural of nouns

In literary Persian the *plural* form (= more than one) of a noun denoting a person is made by adding to the singular form the suffix ان... *-ā́n*; for the plural of a noun not denoting a person the suffix ها... *-hā́* is added. Both suffixes carry the stress of the word:

مهمان *mehmā́n* guest	مهمانان *mehmānā́n* guests		
افسر *afsár* officer	افسران *afsarā́n* officers		
کلید *kelíd* key	کلیدها *kelidhā́* keys		
گزارش *gozāréš* report	گزارشها *gozārešhā́* reports		

Some Iranians still observe this person/not-person distinction, at least in part, when forming the plural of a noun; but in modern everyday Persian there is a tendency to add ‫ها‬... also to many nouns denoting people:

مهمان *mehmán* guest   مهمانها *mehmānhá* guests

افسر *afsár* officer   افسرها *afsarhá* officers

خانمها و آقایان *xānomhā va āqāyān* Ladies and gentlemen

These suffixes are written, and their form is sometimes modified, as follows:

- Whenever it is possible to join ‫ها‬... to its noun in writing, this is correct, though it may also be written detached:

  کتاب *ketāb* book   کتابها\کتاب ها *ketābhā* books

  راه *rāh* road   راهها\راه ها *rāhhā* roads

  but after silent final ه , ‫ها‬... is always written detached (this is a general spelling rule, see 1/15):

  بچه *bacce* child   بچه ها *baccehā* children

- ‫ان‬... is always joined to its noun in writing whenever this is possible:

  مستخدمان *mostaxdemān* employees

- After ا *ā* or و *u,* ‫ان‬... -*ān* becomes ‫یان‬... -*yān*:

  آقا *āqā* gentleman   آقایان *āqāyān* gentlemen

  دانشجو *dānešju* student   دانشجویان *dānešjuyān* students

- silent final ه plus ‫ان‬... -*ān* becomes ‫گان‬... -*egān* (ه is dropped):

  نویسنده *nevisande* writer   نویسندگان *nevisandegān* writers

  راننده *rānande* driver   رانندگان *rānandegān* drivers

Colloquial pronunciation. See 2/6. The suffix ‫ان‬... may be pronounced ‹un› in everyday speech.

Three other plural forms borrowed from Arabic and used for words taken from Arabic, survive in literary style, and are used for a few words (as alternatives to plurals in ‫ها‬...\‫ان‬... -*hā/-ān*) in everyday Persian:

- ات... -*át* (stressed). This is the Arabic so-called 'sound feminine' plural. It is added to certain words ending in a consonant and not denoting persons:

حيوان *heivān* animal   حيوانات *heivānāt* animals

With words ending in silent ه... -*e* and ت... -*at*, the final syllable is dropped before the plural suffix is added:

ملاحظه *molāheze* regard   ملاحظات *molāhezāt* regards

حكايت *hekāyat* story   حكايات *hekāyāt* stories

In imitation of the Arabic, this suffix is also attached to some native Persian words denoting things and ending in -*e* + silent ه . The plural takes the form جات...; the ه is sometimes kept in writing, sometimes dropped. The pronunciation for both spellings is the same, -*ejāt*:

روزنامه *ruznāme* newspaper

روزنامجات\روزنامه‌جات *ruznāmejāt* newspapers

ميوه، ميوجات\ميوه‌جات *mive(jāt)* fruit(s)

- ين...\ون... -*ín*/-*ún* (stressed). This is the Arabic so-called 'sound masculine' plural. It is added to certain nouns denoting male persons. After a consonant, the suffix is ين... -*ín*; after ى... -*i* the suffix is ون... -*ún*:

مترجم *motarjem* translator

مترجمين *motarjemin* translators

استعمارى *este'māri* colonialist

استعماريون *este'māriun* colonialists

- the Arabic irregular or so-called 'broken' plural, in which no suffix is added but the word itself changes its shape (similarly to English 'man/men' or 'mouse/mice'):

شخص *šaxs* person   اشخاص *ašxās* persons

موج *mouj* wave   امواج *amvāj* waves

فصل *fasl* season   فصول *fosul* seasons

مسئله *mas'ale* problem مسائل\مسایل *masāel/masāyel* problems

In everyday Persian some of these forms are found in set expressions:

امواج کوتاه\متوسط\بلند *amvāje kutāh/motavasset/boland* short/medium/long waves

Definite and indefinite. The indefinite suffix ی... *-i* and the definite direct-object suffix را *rā* (3/2, 3 above) are used with plural nouns as with singular nouns:

آیا مهمانهایی رسیده اند؟ *āyā mehmānhāi raside and?* Have any guests arrived?

بچه ها(یی) دیدم. *baccehā(i) didam.* I saw (some) children.

بچه ها را دیدم. *baccehā rā didam.* I saw the children.

پسرها و دخترهارا دیدم. *pesarhā o doxtarhā ra didam.* I saw the boys and girls.

کتابها را با خود برده است. *ketābhā rā bā xod borde ast.* He/She has taken the books with him/her.

Collectives. In an English sentence like 'The baby eats egg' we are not specifying one egg or several eggs, merely the idea 'egg' in general, for which we use the singular form of the noun, as a collective noun. Persian uses this device much more commonly than English, especially for general statements:

آن گربه موش نمی گیرد. *ān gorbe muš nemi girad ‹nemi gire›*. That cat doesn't catch mice ('mouse').

همه اش دروغ است. *hamaš doruq ast ‹e›*. It's all lies ('a lie').

این پسر کشتی دوست دارد. *in pesar kašti dust dārad.* This boy likes ships.

سیب می فروشند؟ *sib mi forušand?* Do they sell apples?

* colloquial pronunciation, see 2/6.

Using a noun collectively transforms it from *countable* to *uncountable* (see 3/2 above); hence we do not attach the indefinite suffix ی... *-i* to a collective. Compare the sentence given above (about the cat) with

آن گربه موشی نمی گیرد. *ān gorbe muši nemi girad ‹nemi gire›.*
That cat doesn't catch a (single) mouse.

Examine also

اینها پیچ هستند. *inhā pic hastand* These are screws.

in which the subject (اینها) and the verb (هستند) are plural. But the word پیچ *pic* 'screw' which is the complement (5/6) of the verb is collective and therefore singular in form.

Although translated with an English plural, the Persian noun stands in the basic singular form. In this meaning it is seen as neither definite nor indefinite, but general, and typifying all its kind.

5 . اضافه *ezāfe* with nouns

The suffix known as the اضافه *ezāfe*, the writing and pronunciation of which are explained in Appendix II, is used to connect two nouns in certain relationships.

Possessive structure. The first such relationship can be called the *possessive structure*. Examine:

کتابها *ketābhā* books, شاگرد *šāgerd* pupil:

کتابهای شاگرد *ketābháye šāgerd* the pupil's books
('the books of the pupil')

کار *kār* work, دانشجویان *dānešjuyān* students:

کار دانشجویان *káre dānešjuyān* the students' work

خانه *xāne* house, مدیر *modir* director:

خانهٔ مدیر *xānéye modir* the director's house
('the house of the director')

صندلی *sandali* chair, پرویز *parviz* Parviz:

صندلی پرویز *sandalíye parviz* Parviz' chair

The 'possessed' noun stands first and carries the *ezāfe* suffixed to it; the 'possessor' noun follows, observing the formula 'the books of the pupil'.

In the examples given above the *ezāfe* is shown in bold type in transcription; it never has any effect on the stress of the word.

The term 'possessive structure' is merely one of convenience. The association between the two nouns may be something other than possession:

كليد *kelid* key, در *dar* door:

كليد در *kelide dar* the key of/to the door

كارگر *kārgar* workman, شكت *šerkat* company:

كارگر شركت *kārgare šerkat* a company workman

راه *rāh* road, فرودگاه *forudgāh* airport:

راه فرودگاه *rāhe forudgāh* the airport road

بودجه *budje* budget, حكومت *hokumat* government:

بودجهٔ حكومت *budjeye hokumat* the government('s) budget

دانشجويان *dānešjuyān* students, دانشكده *dāneškade* faculty:

دانشجويان دانشكده *dānešjuyāne dāneškade*
the faculty students

The 'possessor' noun may be a long infinitive (5/2):

نوشتن *neveštan* to write, عددها *adadhā* figures:

نوشتن عددها *neveštane adadhā* the writing of figures

The *ezāfe* can be repeated, in a 'string'; further, any noun in the expression may have a demonstrative adjective (see 3/12 below):

بودجهٔ حكومت كويت *budjeye hokumate koveit*
the Kuwait Government('s) budget

كار دانشجويان اين دانشكده *kāre dānešjuyāne in dāneškade*
the work of the students of this faculty

رئيس آن كشتى *raise ān kašti* the captain of that ship

In an *ezāfe* construction, the nouns are usually understood to be definite or indefinite as they stand, depending on the context. The 'possessor' noun may be made clearly indefinite with the indefinite suffix (3/2 above) if necessary, but not the 'possessed' noun, since this suffix may not interrupt the *ezāfe*:

نام دانشجويى *nāme dānešjui* some student's name

نمرهٔ ماشینی *nomreye māšini* a car number

The *ezāfe* is not used in expressions of measurement such as 'a kilo of sugar', 'a cup of tea'; see 9/8 for these.

Apposition. The second use of the *ezāfe* with nouns is to link two nouns which are in *apposition*, i.e. the same in identity. The *ezāfe* is attached to the first noun:

خیابان حافظ *xiābāne hāfez* Hafiz Street

شهر قزوین *šahre qazvin* the city of Qazvin

The commonest form of apposition is with آقا\خانم *āqā/xānom* 'Mr, Mrs, Miss' and the person's name or further title:

خانم نوشزاد *xānome nušzād* Mrs/Miss Noushzad

آقای بهروزی *āqāye behruzi* Mr Behrouzi

آقای سفیر *āqāye safir* Mr Ambassador

The *ezāfe* also connects a person's given name and family name:

عباس هادیان *abbāse hādiān* Abbas Hadian

The *ezāfe* is not normally used with other titles or professions followed by the name, even though there is apposition:

دکتر همایون *doktor homāyun* Dr Homayoun

استاد طباطبایی *ostād tabātabāi* Professor Tabatabai

In using these titles when speaking to the person, we use *vocative stress* on the title, for which see 2/5:

سلام آقای منوچهری *salām áqāye manucehri*
Hello, Mr Manuchehri

را *rā* **with the *ezāfe*.** The direct-object suffix را *rā* (3/3 above) may not interrupt the *ezafe* construction. را *ra* appears once, at the end of the expression:

برادر عباس را می‌شناسید؟ *barādare abbās rā mi šenāsid?*
Do you know Abbas' brother?

آقای صبوری را ندیده ام. *āqāye saburi rā nadide am.*
I didn't see/haven't seen Mr Sabouri.

آیا قصه‌های هدایت را خوانده اید؟ *āyā qessehāye hedāyat rā*
xānde id? Have you read the stories of Hedayat?

اصفهان، مسجد امام (مسجد شاه)

esfahān - masjede emām (masjede šāh)
Isfahan - Imam Mosque (King's Mosque)

6. Adjectives - general

An adjective is a word describing (the grammatical term is 'qualifying') a noun (3/1 above) or a pronoun (4/1). Most of the adjectives examined in this chapter are simple adjectives, i.e. not derived from other parts of speech.

Simple adjectives are normally stressed on the last syllable:

کوچک *kucék* small

بزرگ *bozórg* big

See 5/20 and 11/3 for the derivation of adjectives from other parts of speech, and for compound adjectives.

Any adjective may be used as a noun if the meaning permits it:

فقیر *faqir* poor *or* poor person/man/woman

جوان *javān* young *or* young person/man

47

7. Adjective used as complement

One use of the adjective is as a complement (see 5/6) of the verb:

این پدر مهربان است. *in pedar mehraban ast.* This father is kind.

این کار آسان نیست. *in kār āsān nist.* This task is not easy.

(او) زود مریض شد. *(u) zud mariz šod.* She quickly became ill.

مسئله خیلی سخت به نظر می‌آید. *mas'ale xeili saxt be nazar mi āyad.* The problem seems very difficult.

من چنین اقدامی را لازم شمردم. *man conin eqdāmi rā lāzem šomordam.* I considered such a measure necessary.

In a sentence of this kind, the adjective may qualify a noun or a pronoun (see 4/1), including an implied pronoun.

8. Attributive adjectives

An adjective not used as a complement (see 3/7 above) is said to be *attributive*; in the English expression 'a good book' the adjective 'good' is used attributively. An attributive adjective always qualifies a noun, not a pronoun (see 4/1). In English an attributive adjective usually precedes its noun; in Persian it almost always follows its noun. When the noun is used in its basic form (i.e. without the indefinite suffix ی... -*i*, 3/2 above), it carries the suffix called the *ezāfe*, explained in Appendix II. Examine:

کتاب خوب *ketābe xub* a/the good book

کتابهای خوب *ketābhāye xub* (the) good books

اقدام فوری *eqdāme fouri* an/the urgent measure

میوهٔ تازه *miveye tāze* (the) fresh fruit

صندلی چرمی *sandaliye carmi* a/the leather chair

پاروی آهنی *pāruye āhani* an/the iron spade

The *ezāfe* is printed bold in the transcription of these examples; it does not carry any stress, nor does it affect the stress of the word. More than one adjective may be used in this manner, each element in the structure being linked to the next with the *ezāfe*:

خانهٔ بزرگ نو *xāneye bozorge nou* a/the big new house

48

پاروی کهنهٔ آهنی *pāruye kohneye āhani* a/the old iron spade

The structure of <u>noun + adjective</u> is usually understood as either definite or indefinite, according to context. If indefiniteness is emphasised, then one of two devices is used:

- The indefinite suffix ی... is added to the adjective (or the last adjective if there are more than one). If the adjective already ends in ی... -*i* nothing is added:

  کتاب خوبی *ketābe xubi* some good book

  خانهٔ بزرگ نویی *xāneye bozorge noui* some big new house

  صندلی چرمی *sandaliye carmi* some leather chair

- The indefinite suffix ی... is added to the noun, with no *ezāfe*:

  کتابی خوب *ketābi xub* some good book

  خانه‌ای کوچک *xānei kucek* some small house

With this form, we link a series of adjectives with و pronounced *o*, or with *ezāfe*:

خانه‌ای بزرگ و قشنگ *xānei bozorg o qašang*
some beautiful big house

پارویی کهنهٔ آهنی *pārui kohneye āhani*
some old iron spade

Direct object. When appropriate, the noun-and-adjective expression takes the direct-object suffix را *rā* (see 3/3). The suffix is added after the whole expression:

فرهنگ فارسی را گم کرده ام. *farhange fārsi rā gom karde am.*
I have lost the Persian dictionary.

آن دفتر کوچک را کجا گذاشتید؟ *ān daftare kucek rā kojā gozaštid?* Where did you put that small notebook?

Adverbs with adjectives. An adverb (see 7/1) modifying an attributive adjective precedes the adjective. It is one of the few things permitted to interrupt the *ezāfe*:

مرد بسیار بلند *marde besyār boland* the very tall man

مرد بسیار بلندی *marde besyār bolandi* a/some very tall man

جملهٔ کمی کوتاه *jomleye kami kutāh*
a/the somewhat short sentence

چمدانهای خیلی سنگین *camedānhāye xeili sangin*
the very heavy suitcases

Preceding adjective. The adjective پیر *pir* 'old' (of people) usually *precedes* the nouns مرد *mard* 'man' and زن *zan* 'woman', with no *ezafe*:

پیر مرد ، پیر زن *pir mard, pir zan* old man, old woman

9 . Comparative adjectives

The comparative form of the adjective ('bigger', 'more beautiful') is made by suffixing تر... *-tár* (which takes the stress of the word) to the so-called *positive* or basic form of the adjective. The suffix is joined to the adjective in writing if this is possible:

بزرگ *bozórg* big		بزرگتر *bozorgtár* bigger	
قشنگ *qašáng* beautiful		قشنگتر *qašangtár* more beautiful	
بلند *bolánd* tall, high		بلندتر *bolandtár* taller, higher	
کوتاه *kutāh* short		کوتاهتر *kutāhtár* shorter	
کوچك *kucék* small		کوچکتر *kucektár* smaller	
بد *bad* bad		بدتر *badtár* worse	
گران *gerān* expensive		گرانتر *gerāntár* more expensive	
ارزان *arzān* cheap		ارزانتر *arzāntár* cheaper	
تازه *tāzé* fresh		تازه تر *tāzetár* fresher	

A few comparative forms are irregular in that they do not use the common positive form as a base:

خوب *xub* good   بهتر *behtár* better
زیاد *ziād* much   بیشتر *bištár* more (also زیادتر *ziādtar*)

The form بیش *biš* 'more' is also found, as is (in literature) the form به *beh* 'better'.

Like most adjectives shown in this chapter, the ones listed above are simple adjectives, i.e. not derived from another word or form.

The rule for making comparatives applies also to many derived and compound adjectives as well, where the meaning permits it:

باهوش *bāhuš* intelligent   باهوشتر *bāhuštár* more intelligent

جهاندیده *jahāndide*   جهاندیده تر *jahāndidetar*
experienced   more experienced

Derived and compound adjectives are studied in 11/3.

The comparative adjective follows all the rules of the basic or positive adjective when used with a noun (3/7 and 3/8 above), except that by its nature the comparative has indefinite meaning:

این شهر بزرگ است. *in šahr bozorg ast.* This town is big.

آن شهر بزرگتر است. *ān šahr bozorgtar ast.* That town is bigger.

شهر بزرگ *šahre bozorg* the big town

شهر بزرگتر *šahre bozorgtar* a bigger town

عکس قشنگتر *akse qašangtar* a more beautiful photograph

کتاب ارزانتر *ketābe arzāntar* a cheaper book

With a comparative, 'than' is either از *az* or تا *tā*:

• از *az* is by far the commoner of the two. It is used before a noun or pronoun (4/1, 2, 4), with the verb بودن *budan* 'to be', and with any other verb when that verb follows:

ارزانتر از آن یکی ست. *arzāntar az ān yeki st.*
It is cheaper than that one

او جوانتر از من است *u javāntar az man ast.*
He/She is younger than I/me.

A phrase with از can follow the comparative or precede it:

این ارزانتر از آن است. *in arzāntar az ān ast.* ⎤
این از آن ارزانتر است. *in az ān arzāntar ast.* ⎦
This is cheaper than that.

یک کوچکتر از این بده.* *yek kucektar az in bedeh.* ⎤
یکی از این کوچکتر بده.* *yeki az in kucektar bedeh.* ⎦
Give (me) a smaller one than this.

* In this word, final ه is part of the root, and therefore pronounced *h*. See 1/15.

- تا *tā* is used otherwise, i.e. when the next word is neither noun nor pronoun, or when a verb other than بودن precedes. This structure is less common:

به شما بیشتر دادند تا به ما. *be šomā bištar dādand tā be mā*. They gave (to) you more than (to) us.

We also find certain adverbs (see 7/1, 2) used with a comparative. The adverb precedes the adjective, interrupting an *ezāfe* where appropriate. Examples of such adverbs are:

خیلی *xeili* much		کمی *kami* a little	
(به)قدری *(be) qadri* somewhat		نسبتاً *nesbatan* relatively	

خیلی زیادتر پرداخت. *xeili ziādtar pardāxt.*
She paid much more.

کمی پهنتر بود. *kami pahntar bud.* It was a little broader.

این عبارت خیلی روشنتر است. *in ebārat xeili roušantar ast ‹e›*.*
This expression is much clearer.

اجناس نسبتاً گرانتر *ajnāse nesbatan gerāntar*
relatively more expensive goods

* colloquial pronunciation, see 2/6.

as ... as possible. The idiom 'as ... as possible' is expressed in Persian with هر چه + the comparative, هر چه ...تر *har ce -tar.* This formula is most commonly used for adverbs (see 7/3) but is also found with adjectives:

صندوق باید هر چه بزرگتر باشد. *sanduq bāyad har ce bozorgtar bāšad.* The box must be as big as possible.

Equal comparison. Equal comparison is expressed with an abstract noun to represent the adjective, and the *ezāfe*, using the formula shown below:

این به تندی آن است. *in be tondíye ān ast ‹e›.*
This is as fast as that. ('This is to the speed of that.')

یک میخ به طول آن پیچ بدهید. *yek mix be tule ān pic bedehid.*
Give me a nail as long as that screw.

به سنگینیِ آن یکی نیست. *be sanginíye ān yeki nist.*
It isn't as heavy as that one.

11/2 shows the formation of abstract nouns with ی... *-í*.

10. Superlative adjectives

The superlative form of the adjective ('biggest', 'most useful') is made by adding the suffix ین... *-ín* to the comparative ending تر... *-tar*, for which see 3/9 above. The stress shifts on to the *-ín*:

بزرگتر *bozorgtár* bigger	بزرگترین *bozorgtarín* biggest
مفیدتر *mofidtár* more useful	مفیدترین *mofidtarín* most useful
روشنتر *roušantár* clearer	روشنترین *roušantarín* clearest
مشکلتر *moškeltár* more difficult	مشکلترین *moškeltarín* most difficult
بیشتر *bištár* more	بیشترین *bištarín* most
کمتر *kamtár* less	کمترین *kamtarín* least

This applies to most compound and derived adjectives (see 11/3) whose meaning permits it, also:

دولتمندتر *doulatmandtár* wealthier

دولتمندترین *doulatmandtarín* wealthiest

The superlative adjective and its noun are definite in meaning.

When used attributively, the superlative is accompanied by its noun, which it always precedes, with no *ezāfe* (see 3/8 above):

بزرگترین ارتش *bozorgtarin arteš* the biggest army

مفیدترین پیشنهاد *mofidtarin pišnehād* the most useful proposal

این واضحترین جدول است. *in vāzehtarin jadval ast.*
This is the clearest table.

ما قشنگترین شهرهای ایران را دیده ایم.
mā qašangtarin šahrhāye irān rā dide im.
We have seen the most beautiful cities of Iran.

We can use the superlative in attributive use without a noun, but only with singular meaning:

ارزانترین را ببینیم. *arzāntarin/‹arzuntarin› rā bebinim.*
Let's see the cheapest one.

and note the structure <u>superlative + *ezāfe* + plural noun,</u> in which
the superlative again has singular meaning:

مفیدترین پیشنهادها *mofidtarine pišnehādhā*
the most useful (one) of the proposals

مشکلترین حسابها *moškeltarine hesābhā*
the most difficult of the calculations

When the superlative is used as a complement (3/7 above), it is
expressed with the comparative plus از همه *az hame* 'than all'.
Compare the attributive and complementary uses:

{ این تنبلترین جوان بود. *in tambaltarin javān bud.*
This was the laziest youth.

این جوان تنبلتر از همه بود. *in javān tambaltar az hame bud.*
This youth was the laziest ('lazier than all').

{ اینها گرانترین فرشها هستند. *inhā gerāntarin faršhā hastand.* These are the most expensive carpets.

این فرشها از همه گرانترند. *in faršhā az hame gerāntarand.*
These carpets are the most expensive.

11. Possessive adjectives

Possessive adjectives ('my', 'your' etc.) are expressed in two ways
in Persian.

With a personal pronoun. One way is to put the appropriate
personal pronoun (see 4/2) after the possessed noun, connecting
with the *ezāfe* (3/5 above, also Appendix II):

کار من *kāre man* my work ('the work of me')

خانهٔ اوست. *xāneye ust.* It is his/her house

ماشین شما کجاست؟ *māšine šomā kojāst?* Where's your car?

دوستان و دشمنهای ما *dustān va došmanhāye mā*
our friends and enemies

The last example given above shows that the term 'possessive'
used here covers also other associations, as it does in the *possessive*

(noun) *structure.*

These examples are definite. An indefinite possessive is expressed with یکی از *yeki az* 'one of', followed by the noun in the plural, as in English:

یکی از دوستان ما *yeki az dustāne mā* one of our friends

With a suffix. The other way is to add to the noun the appropriate possessive adjective suffix:

Persons	Singular	Plural
1st	م... *-am* my	مان... *-emān* our
2nd	ت... *-et (-at)* your	تان... *-etān* your
3rd	ش... *-eš (-aš)* his/her/its	شان... *-ešān* their

These suffixes do not affect the stress of the noun.

The pronunciatons *-at* and *-aš* are the literary pronunciations, increasingly replaced now by the originally colloquial forms *-et* and *-eš*.

The suffixes are added in this form to a noun ending in a consonant or ی *-i*

دوستم *dústam* my friend   کارتان *kåretān* your work

صندلیم *sandalíam* my chair   کشتیشان *kaštíešān* their boat

After a vowel ا *ā* or و *u*, ...ـی... *-y-* is added before the suffix:

کلیدهایم *kelidhåyam* my keys   پارویش *pārúyeš* his spade

After silent final ه the singular forms are written with initial *alef* and pronounced with *-a-*; the plural forms lose their initial *e* in pronunciation:

خانه‌ام ، خانه‌ات، خانه‌اش *xānéam, xānéat, xānéaš* my, your, his/her house

خانه‌مان ، خانه‌تان، خانه‌شان *xānémān, xānétān, xānéšān* our, your, their house

When the possessed noun has an attributive adjective (3/8 above); the possessive expression (of whichever kind) follows the adjective:

كتاب فارسی من *ketābe fārsiye man* ⎫
كتاب فارسیم *ketābe fārsiam* ⎬ my Persian book

آموزگار سابق او *āmuzgāre sābeqe u* ⎫ his/her former
آموزگار سابقش *āmuzgāre sābeqeš* ⎬ schoolteacher

The direct-object suffix را *rā* (3/3 above), when needed, is added after the whole possessive expression, whichever kind is used. *[man + rā]* becomes مرا *márā*, *[to + rā]* becomes ترا *tórā* (we also encounter the spelling تورا):

شكایت او را قبول نمی‌كنیم. *šekāyate u rā qabul nemi konim.*
We are not accepting his complaint.

خانهٔ مرا خریدند. *xāneye marā xaridand.*
They bought my house.

ماشین ترا كجا پارك كرده اند؟ *māšine torā kojā pārk karde and?* Where have they parked your car?

كتاب او را فراموش كردم. *ketābe u rā farāmuš kardam.* ⎫
كتابش را فراموش كردم. *ketābeš rā farāmuš kardam.* ⎬
I forgot his book.

كتاب فارسی شما را ندیده ام. *ketābe fārsiye šomā rā nadide am.* ⎫
كتاب فارسیتان را ندیده ام. *ketābe fārsietān rā nadide am.* ⎬
I have not seen your Persian book.

In general, the two possessive expressions are equally correct alternatives. However, we cannot use the first possessive expression (*ezāfe* + pronoun) when the subject of the verb (4/2, 5/4) and the possessor of the noun are the same. In such a sentence the suffix form must be used for the possessive:

كتابم را به ایشان* دادم. *ketābam rā be išān dādam.*
(not: [... كتاب مرا]) I gave ('to') him/her/them my book.

ماشینت را كجا پارك كرده ای؟ *māšinet rā kojā pārk karde i?*
Where have you parked your car?

نامه را به خانواده اش فرستاد. *nāme rā be xānevādeaš ferestād.* He/She sent the letter to his/her family.

* polite speech, see 12/2.

56

Where the identity of the possessor is obvious, it is common, especially in speech, to omit the possessive completely:

نامه را به خانواده فرستاد. *nāme rā be xānevāde ferestād.*
He/She sent the letter to (his/her) family.

این فقط برای دوستان است. *in faqat barāye dustān ast.*
This is only for (my) friends.

Emphatic forms. Two possessive forms exist which are used for emphasis. The first is مال من، مال تو ... *māle man, māle to* (etc.) (from the noun مال *māl* 'property'), which is placed after the possessed noun with a connecting *ezāfe*:

کتاب مال شما را گرفت. *ketābe māle šomā rā gereft.*
She took *your* book.

کلاه مال من اینجاست. *kolāhe māle man injāst. My* hat's here.

See 4/5 for مال *māle* in sentences such as 'Mine is ...', 'It's mine/yours' (etc.).

The second emphatic form is the use of the pronoun خود *xod* 'oneself' in place of من، تو *man, to* (etc.) after the *ezāfe*. Because of its meaning, this form is used only when the subject of the verb and the possessor of the noun are the same. In speech it is usual to add the possessive suffix as well:

کتاب خود (م) را به ایشان دادم. *ketābe xod(am) rā be išān dādam.I* gave him/her *my*/my own book.

In literary Persian the use of خود for the possessive is obligatory when both the subject of the verb and the possessor of the noun are the same *3rd* person (او، آن، ایشان، آنها). In this usage there is no emphatic meaning:

کتاب خود را به من داد. *ketābe xod rā be man dād.*
He gave me his book.

کلاه خود را گم کرده است. *kolāhe xod rā gom karde ast.*
He has lost his hat.

کتاب او را) *ketābe u rā* and کلاه او را *kolāhe u rā* in these sentences would mean 'someone else's book', 'someone else's hat').

But in modern everyday style, and in speech, the 3rd-person suffixed form

کتابش را به من داد. *ketābeš rā be man dād.*

کلاهش را گم کرده است. *kolāhes rā gom karde ast.*

is common and accepted; خود is necessary only when emphasis is required.

Literary Persian also has the word خویش *xiš* which can be used instead of خود in all contexts.

See 1/13 for the pronunciation of خود and خویش , and see 4/8 for خود as a pronoun.

شهر بم باستان *šahre bame bāstān*
The ancient city of Bam

12. Demonstrative adjectives

The demonstrative adjectives ('this', 'that' etc.) are:

این *in* this, these آن *ān* that, those

همین *hámin* this/these very همان *hámān* that/those very

چنین *conin* such (a), ... like this چنان *conān* such (a),
... like that

58

These words precede the noun or noun expression which they qualify, without *ezāfe* (see 3/8):

آیا این شخص را می‌شناسید؟ *āyā in šaxs rā mi šenāsid?*
Do you know this person?

آن ساختمانهای بزرگ *ān sāxtemānhāye bozorg*
those big buildings

همان ترجمه است. *hámān tarjome ast.* It is that very translation.

آن افسرها را نمی‌شناسم. *ān afsarhā rā nemi šednāsam.*
I don't know those officers

این نامه را دیده اید؟ *in nāme rā dide id?*
Have you seen this letter?

چنین اسبهای قشنگی تا حالا دیده اید؟
conin asbhāye qašangi tā hālā dide id?
Have you ever ('till now') seen such beautiful horses?

همین is also the commonest way to express 'the same'; in this meaning it loses its connotation 'this':

همین کتاب را خرید. *hámin ketāb rā xarid.*
He bought the same book.

Note that the stress on both همین *hámin* and همان *hámān* falls on *hám-*.

13. Interrogative adjectives

Important interrogative adjectives are:

کدام *kodām ‹kodum›* which   چه *ce* what

چند *cand* how much, how many   کی *ki* whose

چطور\چگونه\چه جور\چه نوع
cetour, cegune, ce jur, ce nou' what kind of

These are used as follows:

- All of them except کی *ki* precede the noun which they qualify, without *ezāfe* (see 3/8):

کدام کتاب...؟ *kodām ketāb...?* which book...?

چطور\چکونه\چه جور\چه نوع شخصی است؟
cetour/cegune/ce jur/ce nou' šaxsi st?
What kind of a person is she?

- کدام *kodām* (colloquial pronunciation ‹*kodum*›) means 'which' (of a limited or known group). Its noun or noun expression has no indefinite suffix ی... *-i* (3/2 above), and carries the definite direct-object suffix را *rā* (3/3 above) when appropriate:

کدام آموزگار اینطور گفت؟ *kodām āmuzgār intour goft?*
Which teacher said so?

کدام تاریخ را بیشتر دوست دارید؟ *kodām tārix rā bištar dust dārid?* Which date do you prefer?

کدام جنسها را میل دارید؟ *kodām jenshā rā meil dārid?*
Which kinds would you like?

Note also کدام یکی ‹*kodum*› *yeki* 'which one', very common in speech.

See the remark at the end of this paragraph.

- چه *ce* mostly means 'what' (of an unlimited or unkown group) and in this meaning its noun or noun expression always carries the indefinite suffix ی...:

امشب چه فیلمی هست؟ *emšab ce filmi hast?*
What film is there tonight?

چه کتابهایی از همه مفیدترند؟ *ce ketābhāi az hame mofidtarand?* What books are most useful?

When the noun is the direct object of a verb, and its identity is known to one party, it is deemed to be definite and therefore also takes the direct-object suffix را *rā*:

چه چیزهای مفیدی را خریدید؟ *ce cizhāye mofidi rā xaridid?* What useful things did you buy?

See the remark at the end of this paragraph.

- کی *ki* meaning 'whose' follows its noun in the same way as a possessive adjective (3/11 above), with *ezāfe*:

پرونده‌ی کی را گرفتید؟ *parvandeye ki rā gereftid?*
Whose file did you take?

In everyday Persian we may find مال کی *māle ki* for 'whose', when emphasis is required:

پروندهٔ مال کی را گرفتید؟

But مال کی *māle ki* is more correctly used as a *pronoun*, i.e. with no noun; see 4/7.

- چند *cand* 'how much/many' is always followed by a singular noun, which has the definite form but is seen as indefinite. If the noun is concrete and 'countable' (i.e. is tangible, and consists of separable units and not a mass), it is usual in modern Persian to add نفر *nafar* for people and تا *tā* for anything else:

چند وقت ماندند؟ *cand vaqt māndand?*
How long ('how much time') did they stay?

چند نفر مهمان می‌آیند؟ *cand nafar mehmān mi āyand?*
How many guests are coming?

چند تا بشقاب برد؟ *cand tā bošqāb bord?*
How many plates did he take?

چند مرتبه گفته ام که ... *cand martabe gofte am ke ...*
How many times have I said that ...

From this last example we can see that the term 'interrogative' covers also rhetorical questions.

چند نفر with no further noun also means 'how many people', and چند تا with no further noun means 'how many (of the things already mentioned)':

چند نفر را شمردید؟ *cand nafar rā šomordid?*
How many people did you count?

چند تا برد؟ *cand tā bord?* How many did he take?

Everyday Persian often uses تا *tā* for people and for things:

چند تا مهمان می‌آیند؟ *cand tā mehmān mi āyand?*

- چطور، چکونه، چه جور، چه نوع *cetour, cegune, ce jur, ce nou'* 'what kind of': the noun following one of these adjectives carries the indefinite ی... *-i*:

چطور گزارشی بود ؟ *cetour gozāreši bud?*
What kind of report was it?

It is important to differentiate between کدام *kodām* 'which' and چه *ce* 'what' described above:

کدام کتاب را می خوانید ؟ *kodām ketāb rā mi xānid?*
Which book (of a known selection) are you reading?

and: چه کتابی را می خوانید ؟ *ce ketābi rā mi xānid?*
What book (of all the books there are) are you reading?

14. Distributive adjectives

The main distributive adjectives are:

تمام *tamām* all, the whole of	همه *hame* all, all of
هر *har* every, each	بعضی *ba'zi* some
چندین *candin* several	چند *cand* some, a few
چند نفر *cand nafar* some (people)	چند تا *cand tā* some (things)
	هیچ *hic* + negative verb no

These adjectives are used as follows:

- تمام *tamām*, همه *hame* all. With a singular noun, the noun تمام *tamām* 'whole', and with a plural noun the pronoun همه *hame* 'all', are used in possessive structure (3/5 above) to mean 'all (of)':

تمام پول را گرفت. *tamāme pul rā gereft.*
He took all (of) the money.

همهٔ مهمانها رفتند. *hameye mehmānhā raftand.*
All the guests went.

- هر *har* every, each. This adjective precedes its noun without *ezāfe*:

هر شاگرد برنامه ای را دارد. *har šāgerd barnāmei rā dārad.* Every pupil has a programme.

The expression هر یکی *har yeki* 'each one' is common in speech:

هر یکی از آنها وظیفه‌ای را دارد. ‹har yeki az onhā
vazifei rā dāre›. Each one of them has a task.

See 9/2 for هر used with numbers.

- بعضی *ba'zi* some. This is used with plural nouns:

بعضی اشخاص *ba'zi ašxās* some people

بعضی اوقات\وقتها *ba'zi ouqāt/vaqthā*
(on) some occasions, sometimes

- چندین *candin* several, چند *cand* some, a few. These precede their noun, which stands in the singular, despite the plural meaning. There is no *ezāfe*:

چندین مهمان *candin mehmān* several guests

چندین روز مانده اند. *candin ruz mānde and.*
They stayed several days.

چند هفته طول کشید. *cand hafte tul kašid.*
It lasted a few weeks.

See 3/13, fifth indent. After چند it is common to put نفر *nafar* before a noun denoting people, and تا *tā* before a noun denoting anything else:

برای امشب چند نفر مهمان دعوت کرده ایم.
barāye emšab cand nafar mehmān da'vat karde im.
For this evening we have invited a few guests.

چند (تا) کتاب *cand (tā) ketāb* some/a few books

In everyday speech it is common to use چند تا before any noun, including one denoting people:

چند تا مسافر شکایت می‌کنند. *cand tā mosāfer šekāyat mi konand.* Some/A few passengers are complaining.

- هیچ *hic* no. We use either هیچ, or the indefinite suffix ی... *-i* (3/2 above), with a negative verb, to express 'no' in either statements or questions:

هیچ مهمان نمی آید. *hic mehmān nemi āyad.* ⎫ No guest
مهمانی نمی آید. *mehmāni nemi āyad.* ⎬ is coming.

هیچ مهمان نیامده؟ ‹hic mehmān nayumade?› ⎫
مهمانی نیامده؟ ‹mehmāni nayumade?› ⎬
Has no guest come? ⎭

هیچ فرصت نداشتیم. hic forsat nadāštim. ⎫ We had
فرصتی نداشتیم. forsati nadāštim. ⎬ no chance

In literary usage only, هیچ expresses 'any' in non-negative
questions; see also 4/10. In everyday Persian it is replaced
by the indefinite ...ی -i:

شکایتی هست؟ šekāyati hast?
Is there any complaint?

دیگری هست؟ digari hast? Is there any other?

4. Pronouns

1 . General

The customary definition of a pronoun is that it is a word replacing a noun whose identity is known. In fact this is true only of 3rd-person pronouns such as 'he', 'she', 'it' (etc.). For the 1st- and 2nd-person pronouns 'I', 'we' and 'you' and their Persian equivalents there is no corresponding noun; the pronoun is the only expression available.

2 . Subject pronouns

The subject of a verb is that person, creature or thing which peforms the action or experiences the situation indicated by the verb. The pronouns denoting the subject of the verb are:

Persons	Singular	Plural
1st	من *man* I	ما *mā* we
2nd	تو *to* you	شما *šomā* you
3rd	او *u* he/she	ایشان *išān* they (people)
	آن *ān* it	آنها *ānhā* they (people/things)

Several things to note:

- There is no grammatical gender (masculine, feminine) in Persian; او *u* means 'he' or 'she' depending on the context.
- For 'you', the singular form تو *to* is used to address a person to whom one is very close indeed; for any other person the plural form شما *šomā* is used. The use of تو is more restricted than that of its apparent European counterparts 'tu', 'du', 'tú' or 'ты'.

  To an animal or a small child also, we say تو ; to all groups, close or not, we say شما .
- The form آنها *ānhā* is used for 'they' referring to any plural -

people, creatures, places, things, ideas. The plural form ایشان *išān* 'they' is now used as a polite form (12/2) for 'he', 'she', or 'they' for people only:

ایشان چه فرمودند؟ *išān ce farmudand**?
What did he/she/they say ('command')?

- These pronouns can be used as they are to denote the subject of the verb but since the verb clearly shows the person of the subject, the pronoun is usually added only for emphasis or extra clarity; or it may form a one-word answer identifying the subject:

من رفتم. *man raftam.* I went. (It is I who went.)

من نمی روم ، تو برو. ‹*man nemi ram***, *to borou.*›
I'm not going, you go.

کی رفت؟ – او. *ki raft?* - *u.* Who went? - He (did).

- Official and newspaper Persian also has the pronoun وی *vei* for 'he/she'.

* Polite verb form, see 12/4.

** Colloquial pronunciation, see 2/6.

3 . Direct-object pronouns

The direct object of a verb is that party directly affected by the action of the verb. Persian has two groups of direct-object pronouns:

- the first group, more common, is derived from the subject pronouns by adding the direct-object suffix را *rā* (3/3):

Persons	Singular		Plural		
1st	مرا	*marā* me	ما را	*mā rā* us	
2nd	ترا	*torā* you	شما را	*šomā rā* you	
3rd	او را	*u rā* him/her	ایشان را	*išān rā* them (people)	
	آن را	*ān rā* it	آنها را	*ānhā rā* them (people/things)	

66

Note the special forms مرا *mará* and ترا *torá*; the latter can also be written in full, تورا. We also encounter the joined forms آنرا and ایشانرا, though these are now discouraged. Each pronoun has the same connotation of person(s) or thing(s) as its subject counterpart shown in 4/2 above:

شما را ندیدم. *šomá rá nadidam.*
I didn't see you (one or more).

آنها را ندیدم. *ánhá rá nadidam.*
I didn't see them (people/things).

ایشان را ندیدم. *išán rá nadidam.*
I didn't see him/her/them (people).

- the second group, used mainly in everyday speech, consists of suffixes which are identical to the possessive-adjective suffixes shown in 3/11 (م... -*am*, ت... -*et* (-*at*), ش... -*eš* (-*aš*) etc.). They are attached to the verb in the same way as the possessives are attached to the noun, and are unstressed. They do not need or take the direct-object suffix را. The 3rd-person suffixes are the commonest in use:

ندیدمش. *nádidameš.* I didn't see him/her/it.

گرفتمشان. *geréftamešán.* I took them.

When used with a compound verb (5/29), the suffix is attached to the non-verbal element:

آهسته بازش کرد. *áheste bázeš kard.* He opened it slowly.

بیرونش کن! *birúneš kon!* Throw it out!

A pronoun which is the direct object of an infinitive (which is always a long infinitive, see 5/2) is attached to it in the manner of a possessive adjective (3/11), i.e. with *ezáfe*:

از دیدن او تعجب کردم. *az didane u ta'ajjob kardam.*
I was surprised to see ('at the seeing of') him.

پیش از رسیدن آنها شروع نمی کنیم.
piš az rasidane ánhá šoru nemi konim.
We shall not begin before they arrive ('before their arrival').

67

4 . Prepositions with pronouns

Prepositions are defined and explained in Chapter 6. The pronouns used after prepositions fall into two groups:

- the first group is identical to the subject pronouns shown in 4/2 above. The prepositions precede the pronoun in the same way as they precede nouns, subject to the same rules (*ezāfe*/no *ezāfe* etc.):

به من *be man* to me

از او *az u* from him/her

برای شما *barāye šomā* for you

بین آنها *beine ānhā* between them

با ما *bā mā* with us

بدون شما *bedune šomā* without you

در آن *dar ān* in it

پیش ایشان *piše išān* towards him/her/them

- the second group consists of suffixes which are identical to the possessive-adjective suffixes shown in 3/11 (م... *-am*, ت... *-et (-at)*, ش... *-eš (-aš)* etc.). The suffixes are attached only to the prepositions which have an *ezāfe* before a noun; the *ezāfe* is dropped, and if two vowels come together as a result they are separated by ـی *-y-*:

داخلش *dāxeleš* inside it

برایم *barāyam* for me

رویشان *ruyešān* on them

به جایتان *be jāyetān* instead of you

جلویش *jelouyeš* before it

پیششان *pišešān* towards him/her/them

We have also the following common but unwritten colloquial 3rd-person forms, with prepositions not carrying the *ezāfe*:

‹*beš/bešān*› to him/her/it/them

‹azeš/azešān› from him/her/it/them

‹beš begam ci?› What am I to say to him/her?

5. Possessive pronouns

The possessive pronouns ('mine', 'yours', 'his', 'hers' etc.) are made by putting مال *māle* before the subject pronouns. This is the same structure as that used for emphatic possessive adjectives (3/11), but whereas the possessive adjective is accompanied by a noun, the possessive pronoun is not, since it replaces the noun:

مال من است. *māle man ast ‹e›**. It's mine.

مال شما بهتر است. *māle šomā behtar ast ‹e›*. Yours is better.

چرا مال ما را بردند؟ *cerā māle mā rā bordand?* Why did they take ours?

* Colloquial pronunciation, see 2/6.

The possessive with مال *māle* may also be put before a possessor noun (including a proper name), whereupon it corresponds to the English possessive expressed with *'s* or with a phrase such as 'that of' or 'those of'. The 'possessed' noun is not expressed but left implicit:

حکایتتان مضحکتر از مال فروشنده است.

hekāyatetān mozhektar az māle forušande ast.
Your story is funnier than the salesman's/that of the salesman.

ماشین مال تو نیست، مال شرکت است. *māšin māle to nist,*
māle šerkat ‹e›. The car isn't yours, it's the company's.

گزارشتان را خواندم ولی برای مال رضا وقت نداشتم.

gozārešetān rā xāndam vali barāye māle rezā vaqt nadāštam.
I have read your report but I didn't have the time for Reza's.

6. Demonstrative pronouns

The demonstrative pronouns are:

این *in* this   آن *ān* that

اینها *inhā* these   آنها *ānhā* those

Unlike the demonstrative adjectives (3/12), این and آن used as pronouns are made plural where appropriate. You will note that آن and آنها are respectively identical to the subject pronouns for 'it' and 'they'.

این روزنامهٔ دیروز است. *in ruznāmeye diruz ast ‹e›.*
This is yesterday's newspaper.

اینها بهترین افسرهایمان هستند. *inhā behtarin afsarhāyemān hastand.* These are our best officers.

از اینها ارزانتر نداریم. *az inhā arzāntar nadārim.*
We have none ('not') cheaper than these.

The demonstrative adjective همین *hámin* (NB stress) can also stand as a pronoun, i.e. without a noun:

همین نیست. *hámin nist.* It isn't the same.

همین را خواستند. *hamin rā xāstand.* They asked for just this.

7. Interrogative pronouns

Common interrogative pronouns are:

کی\که *ki/ke* who   چه *ce ‹ci›* what

مال کی *māle ki* whose

Several things to note:

- The interrogative pronouns ask questions:

کی آمد؟ *ki āmad ‹umad›?* Who came?

چه شد؟ *ce šod?* What happened ('became')?

They should not be confused with other pronoun forms expressed with the same word in English (e.g. 'the man who said this …', for which see 8/6).

- Of the two words for 'who', که *ke* is used only in writing.
- چه *ce* 'what' has a very common colloquial pronunciation (see 2/6), ‹ci›.
- The interrogative pronoun most commonly stands next to the verb (see also 8/2):

رضا چه گفت؟ *rezā ce ‹ci› goft?* What did Reza say?

آنوقت معلمتان کی بود؟ *ānvaqt mo'allemetān ki bud?*
At that time who was your teacher?

(This is similar to the structure called in this book 'topic and comment', explored more fully in 8/14.)

• کی and چه followed by است 'is' become کیست *kist* 'who is' and چیست *cist* 'what is', each written as one word. Possible colloquial pronunciations are ‹ki e› and ‹ci e›:

آن شخص کیست؟ *ān šaxs kist?* Who is that person?

این کیف مال کیست؟ *in kif māle kist?* Whose is this bag?

این سند چیست؟ *in sanad cist ‹ci e›?*
What is this document?

The forms کی است *kist/ki ast* and چه است *ce ast* are also found.

See 4/5 for a fuller explanation of مال *māle*, and 3/11 for the adjectival use of مال کی *māle ki*.

• The pronouns can be preceded by a preposition (4/4 above), and all but چه are followed by the direct-object suffix را *rā* (3/3) when appropriate (که becomes کرا *kerā*):

این را از کی گرفتید؟ *in rā az ki gereftid?*
Who did you get this from ('From whom...')?

راجع به چه صحبت می‌کرد؟ *rāje be ce sohbat mi kard?*
What did he talk about?

کی را دعوت کردند؟ *ki rā da'vat kardand?*
Whom did they invite?

8. خود *xod*

The pronoun خود *xod* 'oneself' (see 1/13 concerning the pronunciation) is used in everyday speech with pronoun suffixes. These suffixes are the same as the possessive-adjective suffixes shown in 3/11. In written Persian خود is mainly used without suffixes. With or without suffixes, خود is used in two ways as a

71

pronoun:

- Emphatic:

خود(ش) آنطور گفت. xod(eš) āntour goft.
He said so himself.

خود(م) نمی دانم. xod(am) nemi dānam
‹nemi dunam›. Myself, I don't know.

and literary Persian has خود followed by the *ezāfe* in, for example:

خود او بود. xode u bud. It was he himself/she herself.

- Reflexive (i.e. returning to the subject):

خود(ش)را دانا می شمرد. xod(eš) rā dānā mi šomorad.
He thinks ('counts') himself knowledgeable.

برای خود(ش) فکر کرد ... barāye xod(eš) fekr kard ...
He thought to ('for') himself ...

باید از خود(تان) دفاع کنید. bāyad az xod(etān)
defā' konid. You must defend yourself.

9. Reciprocal pronouns

The commonest reciprocal pronouns, both meaning 'each other', are:

یکدیگر yekdigar ‹yekdige›   همدیگر hamdigar ‹hamdige›

They can take a direct-object suffix را rā (3/3), a preposition (4/4 above), or be attached in possessive structure with an *ezāfe* (3/11) as appropriate:

همدیگر را دوست نداشتند. hamdigar rā dust nadāštand.
They did not like each other.

با همدیگر خوب همکاری می کنیم. bā hamdigar xub hamkāri
mikonim. We cooperate well ('with each other').

نام یکدیگر را پیشنهاد کرده اند. nāme yekdigar rā pišnehād
karde and. They have proposed one another's names.

10. Distributive pronouns

The main distributive pronouns are:

هر کس\کسی har kas(i) everyone   همه hame all

هر چیز(ی)\همه چیز\همهاش har ciz(i)/hame ciz/hamaš
everything

کسی kasi anyone/no one*   چیزی cizi anything/nothing*

هیچکس* hickas no one   هیچ چیز* hic ciz nothing

هیچکدام* hickodām none   هیچی* ‹hici› nothing

بعضی ها ba'zi hā some   بعضی از ba'zi az some of

زیاد ziād much/many/a lot   خیلی از xeili az many of

                                کم\کمی kam(i) (a) little/few

چند نفر cand nafar   چند تا cand tā
some (of people)   some (of things)

* with a negative verb

The distributive pronouns are used as follows:

- هر کس\هر کسی har kas(i) everyone,
هر چیز(ی)\همه چیز\همهاش har ciz(i)/hame ciz/hamaš
everything.

These pronouns are all singular:

هر کس\هر کسی آن را می داند. har kas(i) ān rā
mi dānad. Everyone knows that.

هر چیز(ی)\همه چیز\همهاشرا برد. hame ciz(i)/
har ciz/hamaš rā bord. He/She took everything.

همهاش hamaš (N B pronunciation) is also used in its literal
meaning 'all of it':

همهاش خراب شد. hamaš xarāb šod. All of it was spoilt.

هرچیز(ی)\همه چیز\همهاش 'everyone' and هر کس(ی)
'everything' are also used in affirmative statements to
express 'anyone' and anything' respectively:

هر کس\هر کسی می تواند آنطور بگوید. har kas(i)
mi tavānad āntour beguyad. Anybody can say that ('thus').

امروزه هر چیز(ی) ممکن است. emruze har ciz(i) momken
ast ‹e›. Nowadays anything ('everything') is possible.

- همه hame all. This is a plural pronoun referring to people, with no noun:

همه رفتند. *hame raftand.* All went.

همه را می شناسم. *hame rā mi šenāsam.* I know (them) all.

It takes *ezāfe* before another pronoun:

از طرف همهٔ ما *az tarafe hameye mā*
on behalf of all of us

• کس *kasi* anyone, چیزی *cizi* anything. In a non-negative question the indefinite nouns کسی *kasi* "a person' and چیزی *cizi* 'a thing' can mean 'anyone' and 'anything' respectively:

آیا کسی تلفن کرد؟ *āyā kasi telefon kard?*
Did anyone ring up?

چیزی گفت؟ *cizi goft?* Did he/she say anything?

With a negative verb, they mean 'no one' and 'nothing' respectively:

کسی نیامد. *kasi nayāmad.* No one came

چیزی نگفتم. *cizi nagoftam.* I said nothing.

• هیچکدام *hickas* no one, هیچ چیز *hic ciz* nothing, هیچکس *hickodām* none, هیچی ‹hici› nothing. In a negative statement or question, these pronouns are used with a negative verb to express 'no' or 'no-' and 'none'. In this usage, the first two are alternatives to کسی *kasi* and چیزی *cizi* respectively:

کسی\هیچکس تلفن نکرد. *kasi/hickas telefon nakard.*
No one rang up.

کسی\هیچکس تلفن نکرد؟ *kasi/hickas telefon nakard?*
Did no one ring up?

چیزی\هیچ چیز ننوشتم. *cizi/hic ciz nanevestam.*
I wrote nothing.

آیا هیچکدام نمی آید؟ *āyā hickodām nemi āyad?*
Is none (of them) coming?

In colloquial speech, هیچی ‹hici› can replace هیچ چیز *hic ciz* or چیزی *cizi*:

74

هیچی ننوشتم. ‹hici nanevestam.›

هیچی بهتر پیدا نمی کنید. ‹hici behtar peidā nemi konid.›
You won't find any(thing) better.

Note also the short negative answers in everyday language
with هیچ:

کی تلفن کرد؟ - هیچکس. ki telefon kard? - hickas.
Who telephoned? - Nobody.

کدام دکتر را دیدید؟ - هیچکدام.
kodām ‹kodum› doktor rā didid? - hickodām ‹hickodum›.
Which doctor did you see? - None.

چه فرمودید*؟ - هیچ چیز\هیچی. ce farmudid?
- hic ciz/hici. What did you say? - Nothing.

* Polite speech, see 12/4.

- بعضی ها ba'zi hā some, بعضی از ba'zi az some of. These
are indefinite and plural. In بعضی ها the plural suffix is
usually written separately:

بعضی ها دیر رسیدند. ba'zi hā dir rasidand.
Some arrived late.

بعضی ها را نمی شناسم. ba'zi hā rā nemi šenāsam.
There are some I don't know. ('I don't know some'.)

بعضیی ها شکایت کردند. ba'zi hā šekāyat kardand.
Some complained.

بعضی از آنها خراب شدند. ba'zi az ānhā xarāb šodand.
Some of them got spoiled.

- زیاد ziād much, many, a lot, خیلی از xeili az many of,
کم\کمی kam/kami (a) little, (a) few. These pronouns are all
indefinite, singular or plural as the meaning dictates:

چه می گویید که کمی دارید؟ زیاد دارید.
‹ce mi gid ke kami dārid? ziād dārid.›
What are you saying, you've got a little? You've got a lot.

کمی مانده است. kami mānde ast. A little has remained.

خیلی از آنها رفتند. xeili az ānhā raftand.
Many of them went.

- چند نفر *cand nafar* some (of people), چند تا *cand tā* some (of things). These adjectival expressions (3/14) can also be regarded and used as pronouns:

چند نفر غایب هستند. *cand nafar qāyeb hastand.*
Some are absent.

چند تا فروختند. *cand tā foruxtand.* They sold some.

5. Verbs

1. General

A verb is that class of word which denotes an action or situation:

تند دوید . *tond <u>david</u>.* He/She <u>ran</u> fast.

خوشحال بودیم. *xošhāl <u>budim</u>.* We <u>were</u> happy.

نمی‌تواند آن را پیدا کند . *nemi tavānad ān rā <u>peidā konad</u>.* He/She <u>cannot find</u> it.

2. Infinitive

The infinitive is the form of the verb by which it is referred to, and listed in a dictionary. Typical English infinitives are '(to) read' and '(to) run'; the particle 'to' is sometimes added, sometimes not. The Persian infinitive has no such particle.

Persian has two forms of the infinitive; the commoner one, used to identify the verb, is the *long* infinitive, which ends in دن... *-dán* or تن... *-tán*. This ending takes the stress of the word (see 2/5):

خواندن *xāndán* to read (silent و , see 1/13)

دویدن *davidán* to run   کشتن *koštán* to kill

The long infinitive is not only a 'label'. It is also used as a noun naming the activity:

برای بچه‌ها خواندن آسان نیست. *barāye baccehā xāndan āsān nist.* Reading is not easy for children.

خواندن را بسیار دوست دارد . *xāndan rā besyār dust dārad.* She likes reading very much.

برای خواندن وقت ندارم. *barāye xāndan vaqt nadāram.* I have no ('not') time for reading.

A long infinitive which has a direct object (5/6 below) is joined to it with *ezāfe* (Appendix II):

برای خواندن روزنامه وقت ندارم.
barāye xāndane ruznāme vaqt nadāram.
I have no time to read ('for the reading of') the newspaper.

77

به دیدن آنها رفتیم. *be didane ānhā raftim.*
We went to see them.

The *short* infinitive is the same as the long infinitive minus its final
ن... -*an*. It is stressed on its final syllable:

خواند *xānd* to read   دوید *davíd* to run

کشت *košt* to kill

The use of this form is examined in 5/19 and 27 below.

3. Position of the verb

A verb other than an auxiliary verb (5/19 below) usually stands at
the end of its sentence or clause (see 8/4 for the definition of a
clause):

کتاب را خواندم. *ketāb rā xāndam.* I read the book.

آن دانشجو را می‌شناسید؟ *ān dānešju rā mi šenāsid?*
Do you know that student?

تند می نویسد. *tond mi nevisad.* He/She writes fast.

دکان بسته است. *dokkān baste ast.* The shop is closed.

می‌تواند تند بدود. *mi tavānad tond bedavad.*
He/She can run fast.

See 6/6 for an exception to this rule in colloquial language.

4. Agreement

A verb agrees with its *subject* (i.e. the person, creature or thing
performing the action or experiencing the situation indicated by the
verb) in *person* (1st, 2nd or 3rd) and in *number* (singular with
singular, plural with plural). A pronoun subject (4/2) is often
omitted when it is clear from the form of the verb:

(من) اینجا هستم. *(man) inja hastam.* I am here.

شما کجا رفتید؟ *šomā kojā raftid?* Where did you go?

کجا بود؟ *kojā bud?* Where was he/she/it?

ایشان را خوب می‌شناسیم. *išān rā xub mi šenāsim.*
We know them well.

اینجا هستند. *injā hastand.* They are here.

But note:

- In polite speech (see 12/2 and 3) the plural subject pronoun ایشان *išān* has a plural verb even when used to express 'he' or 'she'; the same happens with a singular noun subject denoting a person:

ایشان بلد هستند؟ *išān balad hastand?*
Is he/she informed?

معلم چه فرموده اند؟ *mo'allem ce farmude and?*
What did the teacher say ('command')?

مدیر امروز غایب هستند. *modir emruz qāyeb hastand.*
The director's away today.

- Earlier Persian often has a plural noun denoting things or ideas (not people) with a singular verb:

دکانها بسته بود. *dokkānhā baste bud.*
The shops were ('was') closed.

and this structure survives in some set expressions:

اوقاتش تلخ شد. *ouqāteš talx šod.* He became angry.
('His times (plural) became (singular) bitter')

5 . Simple and compound verbs

We distinguish between simple and compound verbs in Persian.

A simple verb is one whose infinitive (5/2 above) consists of one word:

فهمیدن *fahmidan* to understand   بافتن *bāftan* to weave

کردن *kardan* to do   داشتن *dāštan* to have

رفتن *raftan* to go   آمدن *āmadan* to come

A compound verb consists of a non-verbal part and a simple verb. Typical compound infinitives are:

کار کردن *kār kardan* to work

بر داشتن *bar dāštan* to remove

از بین رفتن *az bein raftan* to disappear

پیش آمدن *piš āmadan* to occur

79

Compound verbs are examined in 5/29 and 30 below. Almost all the verbs described in 5/2 to 28 are simple verbs.

6. Government: subject, complement and object

All verbs have a *subject* (see 4/2 and 5/4 above):

سـیـروس رفت. *sirus raft.* <u>Cyrus</u> went.

کتابم اینجاست. *ketābam injāst.* <u>My book</u> is here.

We can however put Persian verbs into three broad types according to their relationship with other parts of the sentence:

- verbs which have no *object* (i.e. no affected party other than the subject):

اینجا هست. *injā hast.* He is here.

مردند. *mordand.* They died.

بیرون رفته است. *birun rafte ast.* He/She has gone out.

Some verbs with no object have a *complement*, i.e. a further word or expression identifying or describing the subject:

برادرم آموزگار است. *barādaram āmuzgār ast.*
My brother is a teacher.

همکارم مریض شد. *hamkāram mariz šod.*
My colleague fell ('became') ill.

The complement is so called because it completes the meaning of the verb. Almost all verbs of being, seeming or becoming need a complement.

Complements most often take the form of a noun (3/1) or adjective (3/6).

- verbs which have a *direct object* (i.e. a second party directly affected):

آنها را دیدم. *ānhā rā didam.* I saw them.

نامه‌ای نوشت. *nāmei nevešt.* She wrote a letter.

این نویسنده را نمی‌شناسیم. *in nevisande rā nemi šenāsim.*
We don't know this writer.

- verbs which have a *prepositional object* (i.e. a second party affected, but preceded by a preposition, see 6/1):

از من پرسیدند. *az man porsidand.*
They asked ('from') me.

راجع به وضع بین المللی نوشته است.
rāje' be vaz'e beinolmelali nevešte ast.
He has written about the international situation.

In English, the prepositions 'to' and 'for' can often be omitted, making the object look like a direct object. In Persian the preposition cannot be omitted:

به شما چه داده اند؟ *be šomā ce dāde and?*
What did they give ('to') you?

برای پسر خود منزل ساخت. *barāye pesare xod manzel sāxt.* He built ('for') his son a house.

A verb can have both a direct and a prepositional object:

از آنها چه پرسید؟ *az ānhā ce porsid?*
What did he ask them?

(direct object for the person, prepositional object for the thing affected)

هدیه به دوستان دادند. *hadiye be dustān dādand.*
They gave a present to (their) friends.

(direct object for the thing, prepositional object for the person affected)

The relationship of a verb to its complement or object (if any) is called its *government*. A Persian verb does not necessarily have the same government as its nearest English equivalent:

از کسی\از چیزی ترسیدن *az kasi/az cizi tarsidan*
to fear ('from') somebody/something

(direct object in English, prepositional object with از *az* in Persian)

Some verbs cause their direct object to perform the action. These are known as *causative* verbs. They are explained in 11/4.

7. Tenses

A tense is that form of the verb which indicates the time or the context in which the action or situation denoted by the verb occurs. Persian has four simple (i.e. one-word) tenses:

- Past, indicating a completed previous action or situation ('I did'), see 5/8, 9 below.
- Present, indicating a current or impending action or situation ('I do', 'I am doing'), see 5/10-12 below.
- Imperfect, indicating a continuous or repeated previous action or situation ('I was doing'), see 5/13, 14 below.
- Present subjunctive, indicating a possibility ('I may do'), see 5/16, 17 below.

and four common compound tenses (i.e. tenses formed with more than one word):

- Perfect ('I have done'), similar in meaning to the past tense, see 5/21, 22 below.
- Perfect subjunctive, indicating a previous possibility ('I may have done'), see 5/23, 24 below.
- Pluperfect, indicating one previous action or situation preceding another ('I had done'), see 5/25, 26 below.
- Future, indicating an action or situation occurring ahead ('I shall do'), see 5/27, 28 below.

8. Forming the past tense

We form the past tense ('I did') with the

<u>past stem + past personal endings</u>

Past stem. The past stem is easy to form. We remove the final ن... -*an* from the long infinitive (5/2 above):

Infinitive	Past stem
خواندن *xāndan* to read	خواند.... *xānd-* (silent و , 1/13)
آمدن *āmadan* to come	آمد.... *āmad-*
بودن *budan* to be	بود... *bud-*
کشتن *koštan* to kill	کشت... *košt-*

82

رفتن *raftan* to go   رفت... *raft-*

ساختن *sāxtan* to make   ساخت... *sāxt-*

and so on for all verbs in the language.

Personal endings. The personal endings of the past tense are:

Persons	Singular		Plural	
1st	م...	*-am* I	یم...	*-im* we
2nd	ی...	*-i* you	ید...	*-id* you
3rd	...	*-* he/she/it	ند...	*-and* they

See 4/2 for the use of the persons. The 3rd person singular form of the tense ('he', 'she', 'it') has no ending; for this form the past tense is identical to the stem itself.

All past stems and endings, and hence all past tenses, are regular. The past-tense verb is stressed on the last syllable of the past stem, when the verb is affirmative. Typical past tenses:

خواندن *xāndan* to read, past stem خواند... *xānd-* (the stress is shown in this example):

خواندم *xā́ndam*	خواندیم *xā́ndim*
خواندی *xā́ndi*	خواندید *xā́ndid*
خواند *xānd*	خواندند *xā́ndand*

I, you, he, she, it, we, they read (previously)

آمدن *āmadan* to come, past stem آمد... *āmad-*:

آمدم، آمدی، آمد ... *āmadam, āmadi, āmad* (etc.) I (etc.) came;

بودن *budan* to be, past stem بود... *bud-*:

بودم، بودی، بود؛ بودیم، بودید، بودند *budam, budi, bud;*
budim, budid, budand I, he, she, it was; we, you, they were.

So also all other verbs whose past stem ends in د *d.*

کشتن *koštan* to kill, past stem کشت... *košt-* (the stress is shown):

کشتم *kóštam*	کشتیم *kóštim*
کشتی *kóšti*	کشتید *kóštid*
کشت *košt*	کشتند *kóštand*

I, you, he, she, it, we, they killed

رفتن *raftan* to go, past stem ...رفت *raft-*:

... رفتم، رفتی، رفت *raftam, rafti, raft* (etc.) I (etc.) went;

ساختن *sāxtan* to make, past stem ...ساخت *sāxt-*:

... ساختم، ساختی، ساخت *sāxtam, sāxti, sāxt* (etc.) I (etc.) made.

So also all other verbs whose past stem ends in ت *t*.

Colloquial pronunciation. See 2/6. Colloquial pronunciation can be used for the past tense:

- The syllable ...ان... *-ān* in the past stem is often pronounced ‹un› or ‹on›, as elsewhere in the language:

  خواندم. ‹xundam.› I've read (it).

- The past stem ...آمد *āmad* is pronounced colloquially ‹umad-›:

  دیر آمدی. ‹dir umadi›. You're ('You came') late.

  See 5/19 for the past stem...توانست *tavānest-* pronounced colloquially ‹tunest-›.

- The personal endings ...ید *-id* and ...ند *-and* are pronounced colloquially *-in* and *-an* respectively. Not all speakers use these two variants.

Negative. The negative of the past tense ('I did not do') is formed by adding the negative prefix ...نَ *ná-* to the affirmative verb. This prefix always takes the stress of the word:

نخواندیم *náxāndim.* we did not read

نبودم *nábudam* I was not

نرفت *náraft* he/she did not go

When the past stem begins with a vowel *ā, a* or *o*, the negative prefix becomes...نی *náy-*:

- The combination *náyā-* is written with no *madde*:

  آمدند *āmadand* they came

  نیامدند *náyāmadand* they did not come

  آوردم *āvordam* I brought

  نیاوردم *náyāvordam* I did not bring

- The combinations *náya-* and *náyo-* are written without *alef*:

انداختیم *andāxtim* we threw

نینداختیم *náyandāxtim* we did not throw

افتاد *oftād* it fell

نیفتاد *náyoftād* it did not fall

The combination *nái-* occurs in the only Persian verb beginning with the vowel ـایـ... *i-*, ایستادن *istādan* 'to stand', 'to stop'. With this verb the *alef* is retained:

ایستادم *istādam* I stood/stopped

نایستادم *náistādam* I did not stand/stop

This *alef* is merely a spelling device, and is not pronounced *[ā]*. Some Iranians detach the prefix from this verb, writing it نه :

نه‌ایستادم *ná istādam*

For the past tense of *compound verbs*, see 5/29.

9 . Using the past tense

The past tense is used similarly to the English past tense, i.e. for single previous completed actions or situations which are not deemed to have any effect on, or any relevance to, the present:

او را دیدم. *u rā didam.* I saw him.

آنجا نبودیم. *ānjā nábudim.* We were not there.

کجا رفتید؟ *kojā raftid?* Where did you go?

Two other less obvious uses:

- in certain clauses of time relating to the future; see 8/9, first indent.

- in expressions such as the following, especially common in everyday speech:

آمدم دیگر. (colloquially) ‹*āmadam dige›.*
All right, I'm coming.

رفتم. *raftam.* I'm off.

تو برو، من آمدم. *to borou, man āmadam.*
You go (first), I'll follow.

The past tense is not normally used for a previous action which was continuous or repeated (see 5/13, 14), or for a previous action having an effect on the present situation (see 5/21, 22).

For a previous action or situation which was interrupted by another previous event, Persian also uses the past tense where English expresses it differently:

وقتیکة او رسید من چند سال آنجا بودم.

vaqtike u rasid man cand sāl ānjā budam.
When she arrived I had been ('was') there for some years.

در بازار کرمان *dar bāzāre kermān* In Kerman Bazaar

10. Forming the present tense

We form the present tense ('I do', 'I am doing') with the

present prefix + present stem + present personal endings

Present prefix. The present prefix is می *mi*. It is commonly written detached from the verb. The present prefix is stressed when it is the only prefix (i.e. when the verb is affirmative): *mí*.

Present stem. To make the present stem of all verbs whose long infinitive (5/2 above) ends in ...ندن *-ndan* we remove the ending ...دن *-dan* from that infinitive:

Infinitive	Present stem
خواندن* *xāndan* to read	خوانـ... *xān-*
ماندن *māndan* to remain	مانـ... *mān-*
راندن *rāndan* to drive	رانـ... *rān-*

* silent و , see 1/13.

We make the present stem of many verbs whose long infinitive ends in ...ادن *-ādan* or ...یدن *-idan* by removing the ending ...ادن *-ādan* or ...یدن *-idan* from that infinitive:

افتادن *oftādan* to fall	افتـ... *oft-*
ایستادن *istādan* to stand/stop	ایستـ... *ist-*
دویدن *davidan* to run	دو... *dav-*
خریدن *xaridan* to buy	خر... *xar-*
پوشیدن *pušidan* to wear	پوشـ... *puš-*
خوابیدن *xābidan* to sleep	خوابـ... *xāb-*

A few verbs with long infinitive ending ...تن *-tan* make their present stem by dropping the ending ...تن *-tan* from that infinitive:

کشتن *koštan* to kill	کشـ... *koš-*
بافتن *bāftan* to weave	بافـ... *bāf-*

These are all regular present stems.

For most remaining verbs the present stem is irregular and has to be learned with the verb. Some irregulars can be grouped, having similar stems. Appendix I lists common irregular present stems.

Examples of such present stems are:

Other long infinitives ending ...یدن\ادن... -ādan/-idan:

دادن dādan to give	ده... deh-
آفریدن āfaridan to create	آفرین... āfarin-
چیدن cidan to set	چین... cin-
شنیدن šenidan to hear	شنو... šenav-
دیدن didan to see	بین... bin-

Long infinitives ending ...ودن -udan:

| نمودن namudan to show | نما... namā- |
| فرمودن farmudan to command | فرما... farmā- |

Other long infinitives ending ...دن -dan:

مردن mordan to die	میر... mir-
شدن šodan to become	شو... šav-
شمردن šomordan to count	شمار... šomār-
بردن bordan to take/carry	بر... bar-
آمدن āmadan to come	آ... ā-
کردن kardan to do	کن... kon-
آوردن āvordan/āvardan to bring	آر... ār-, also regular آور... āvar-

Other long infinitives ending ...تن -tan:

ساختن sāxtan to make	ساز... sāz-
انداختن andāxtan to throw	انداز... andāz-
فروختن foruxtan to sell	فروش... foruš-
گذشتن gozaštan to pass	گذر... gozar-
گذاشتن gozāštan to put	گذار... gozār-
نشستن nešastan to sit	نشین... nešin-
بستن bastan to tie, to close	بند... band-
گفتن goftan to say	گو... gu-
رفتن raftan to go	رو... rav-

and many others

Principal parts. We can conveniently refer to any verb, regular or irregular, by its two 'principal parts', i.e. the long infinitive and the present stem, so:

خریدن خر... *xaridan xar-* to buy   گفتن گو... *goftan gu-* to say

since from these parts any form of any verb can be derived (with the exception of one verb only, بودن *budan* 'to be', for which see 5/11).

Present personal endings. The present-tense personal endings used *when the present stem ends in a consonant* are the same as those of the past tense (5/9 above), except the 3rd person singular:

Persons	Singular	Plural
1st	م... *-am* I	یم... *-im* we
2nd	ی... *-i* you	ید... *-id* you
3rd	د... *-ad* he/she/it	ند... *-and* they

See 4/2 for the use of the persons.

The present-tense verb is assembled in the order <u>prefix + stem + ending</u>. Typical present tenses with the stem ending in a consonant:

<u>Regular stems:</u>

خواندن خان... *xāndan xān-* to read (the stress is shown in this example):

می خوانم	*mí xānam*	می خوانیم	*mí xānim*
می خوانی	*mí xāni*	می خوانید	*mí xānid*
می خواند	*mí xānad*	می خوانند	*mí xānand*

I read/am reading (etc.)

افتادن افت... *oftādan oft-* to fall:

می افتم	*mi oftam*	می افتیم	*mi oftim*
می افتی	*mi ofti*	می افتید	*mi oftid*
می افتد	*mi oftad*	می افتند	*mi oftand*

I fall/am falling (etc.)

ایستادن ایست... *istādan ist-* to stand, to stop:

می‌ایستم *mi istam*   می‌ایستیم *mi istim*
می‌ایستی *mi isti*   می‌ایستید *mi istid*
می‌ایستد *mi istad*   می‌ایستند *mi istand*

I stand, stop/am standing, stopping (etc.)

خریدن خر... *xaridan xar-* to buy:

می‌خرم *mi xaram*   می‌خریم *mi xarim*
می‌خری *mi xari*   می‌خرید *mi xarid*
می‌خرد *mi xarad*   می‌خرند *mi xarand*

I buy/am buying (etc.)

کشتن کش... *koštan koš-* to kill:

می‌کشم *mi košam*   می‌کشیم *mi košim*
می‌کشی *mi koši*   می‌کشید *mi košid*
می‌کشد *mi košad*   می‌کشند *mi košand*

I kill/am killing (etc.)

Irregular stems:

کردن کن... *kardan kon-* to do (the stress is shown in this example):

می‌کنم *mí konam*   می‌کنیم *mí konim*
می‌کنی *mí koni*   می‌کنید *mí konid*
می‌کند *mí konad*   می‌کنند *mí konand*

I do/am doing (etc.)

دیدن بین... *didan bin-* to see:

می‌بینم *mi binam*   می‌بینیم *mi binim*
می‌بینی *mi bini*   می‌بینید *mi binid*
می‌بیند *mi binad*   می‌بینند *mi binand*

I see (etc.)

بستن بند... *bastan band-* to tie, to close:

می‌بندم *mi bandam*   می‌بندیم *mi bandim*
می‌بندی *mi bandi*   می‌بندید *mi bandid*
می‌بندد *mi bandad*   می‌بندند *mi bandand*

I tie, close/am tying, closing (etc.)

انداختن انداز ...انداز andāxtan andāz- to throw

می اندازیم mi andāzim	می اندازم mi andāzam
می اندازید mi andāzid	می اندازی mi andāzi
می اندازند mi andāzand	می اندازد mi andāzad

I throw/am throwing (etc.)

The present-tense personal endings used *when the present stem ends in a vowel* are the same as those for stems ending in a consonant, except that the letter ﻯ *ye* is put before the endings. Before endings beginning -*a*- the *ye* is sounded -*y*-, before endings beginning -*i*- the *ye* is silent (see 2/4):

Persons	Singular	Plural
1st	یم... -*yam* I	ییم... -*im* we
2nd	یی... -*i* you	یید... -*id* you
3rd	ید... -*yad* he/she/it	یند... -*yand* they

Typical present tenses with stems (all irregular) ending in a vowel (which is always either ﺁ *ā* or ﻭ *u*):

آمدن آ... āmadan ā- to come:

می آییم mi āim	می آیم mi āyam
می آیید mi āid	می آیی mi āi
می آیند mi āyand	می آید mi āyad

I come/am coming (etc.)

نمودن نما... namudan namā- to show:

می نماییم mi namāim	می نمایم mi namāyam
می نمایید mi namāid	می نمایی mi namāi
می نمایند mi namāyand	می نماید mi namāyad

I show/am showing (etc.)

گفتن گو... goftan gu- to say:

می گوییم mi guim	می گویم mi guyam
می گویید mi guid	می گویی mi gui
می گویند mi guyand	می گوید mi guyad

I say/am saying (etc.)

Older spellings یئ... for یی... -*i*, یئیم... for ییم... *im*, یئید... for یید...

91

-id, are still found. We need to be able to recognise them:

(می آئیم) mi āim   (می گوئید) mi guid

We also encounter the present prefix mi joined in writing to the verb, though this is older spelling and is now discouraged. When the present stem begins with a consonant, the spelling in this style of writing is obvious:

(میخوانم) mixānam I read   (میکنیم) mikonim we do

می نما ییم for (مینمائیم\مینماییم) minamāim we show

When the present stem begins with a vowel, the beginning of the present tense in this style of writing is as follows:

- the combination *míā-* is written with no *madde*:

  آمدن آ... āmadan ā- to come:

  میایم، میایی\میائی... miāyam, miāi (etc.)
  I come/am coming (etc.)

- the combinations *mía-* and *mío-* are written without *alef*:

  انداختن انداز... andāxtan andāz- to throw:

  میندازم، میندازی ... miandāzam, miandāzi (etc.)
  I throw/am throwing

  افتادن افتـ... oftādan oft- to fall:

  میفتم، میفتی ... mioftam, miofti (etc.)
  I fall/am falling (etc.)

For the only verb with infinitive and stem beginning with ای... *i-*, i.e. ایستادن ایستـ... *istādan ist-* 'to stand, to stop', the prefix is always written separately, as shown earlier.

Colloquial pronunciation. See 2/6. The impact of colloquial pronunciation on the present tense is felt in several areas:

- The syllable ...ـان... *ān* in the present stem (regular or irregular) can be pronounced colloquially ‹un›, ‹on›, as it can in most words.
- Many irregular present stems are shortened in pronunciation.
- The personal ending د... *-ad* is pronounced ‹-e› after a

consonant.

- The personal endings ...بد ‎ -id and ...ند ‎ -and are pronounced colloquially ‹-in› and ‹-an› respectively. Not all speakers use these two variants.

The pronunciation of the present prefix *mi*, and the spelling and stress of the whole verb, do not change. Here are those present stems shown in this paragraph which have a colloquial pronunciation:

Verb		Colloquial present stem
...خواندن خوانـ ‎	*xāndan xān-* to read	‹xun-›
...ماندن مانـ ‎	*māndan mān-* to remain	‹mun-›
...راندن رانـ ‎	*rāndan rān-* to drive	‹run-›
...دادن دهـ ‎	*dādan deh-* to give	‹d-›
...شدن شوـ ‎	*šodan šav-* to become	‹š-›
...آمدن آ ‎	*āmadan ā-* to come	‹ā› (see below)
...گفتن گوـ ‎	*goftan gu-* to say	‹g-›
...رفتن روـ ‎	*raftan rav-* to go	‹r-›
...گذاشتن گذار ‎	*gozāštan gozār-* to put	‹zār-›
...گذشتن گذرـ ‎	*gozaštan gozar-* to pass	‹zar-›

Annex I lists irregular present stems, with standard and colloquial pronunciation.

Examples of present tenses in colloquial pronunciation (in transcription only):

...ماندن مانـ ‎ *māndan mān/‹mun-›* to remain:

‹mi munam, mi muni, mi mune; mi munim, mi munin, mi munan›

...دادن دهـ ‎ *dādan deh-/‹d-›* to give:

‹mi dam, mi di, mi de; mi dim, mi din, mi dan›

...شدن شوـ ‎ *šodan šav/‹š-›-* to become:

‹mi šam, mi ši, mi še; mi šim, mi šin, mi šan›

...گفتن گوـ ‎ *goftan gu-/‹g-›* to say:

‹mi gam, mi gi, mi ge; mi gim, mi gin, mi gan›

رفتن رو... *raftan rav-/‹r-›* to go:

‹*mi ram, mi ri, mi re; mi rim, mi rin, mi ran*›

گذاشتن گذار... *gozāštan gozār-/‹zār›* to put:

‹*mi zāram, mi zāri, mi zāre; mi zārim, mi zārin, mi zāran*›

In آ... آمدن *āmadan ā-* 'to come'; *-āya-* becomes ‹*-ā-*›:

‹*mi ām, mi āi, mi ād; mi āim, mi āin, mi ān*›

Negative. The negative of the present tense ('I do not do', 'I am not doing') is formed by adding the negative prefix نـ... *ne-* to the می *mi* of the affirmative verb. The two prefixes are written together. The 'literary' pronunciation of this double prefix is *námi*, but the prononciaton *némi*, formerly only colloquial, is now used even in formal speech for the present tense. However pronounced, the negative prefix always takes the stress of the word:

نمی روم. *némi ravam/námi ravam*. I am not going.

نمی افتد. *némi oftad/námi oftad*. It is not falling/will not fall.

To have. The verb داشتن دار... *dāštan dār-* 'to have' forms its present tense regularly from its stem, but it does not have the present prefix. The stress is on the stem:

دارم	*dáram*	داریم	*dárim*
داری	*dári*	دارید	*dárid ‹dárin›*
دارد	*dárad ‹dáre›*	دارند	*dárand ‹dáran›*
	I have (etc.)		

dárad, *dárid* and *dárand* can be pronounced colloquially ‹*dáre, dárin, dáran*› respectively.

Negative is with نـ... *ná-*:

ندارم، نداری، ندارد؛ نداریم، ندارید، ندارند

nádāram, nádāri, nádārad; nádārim, nádārid, nádārand
I do not have (etc.)

To be. بودن باش... *budan bāš-* 'to be' is irregular in the present tense and is examined in 5/11 below.

For the present tense of *compound verbs*, see 5/29.

11. Forming the present tense: 'to be'

The present tense ('I am, you are' etc.) of the verb بودن باش‍...
buḍan bāš- 'to be' has three forms, the commonest two of which
are irregular.

First form. The first form of the present tense is:

Persons	Singular	Plural
1st	م\ام‍... -am/ am	یم\ایم‍... -im/ im
2nd	ی\ای‍... -i/ i	ید\اید‍... -id/ id
3rd	ست\است‍... -st/ ast	ند\اند‍... -and/ and
	I am (etc.)	

Several things to note about this form:

- *All the forms except the 3rd person singular* (او\آن) *are most
  often joined to the previous word when that word ends in a
  consonant:*

فقیرم. *faqiram.* I am poor.

مهربانی\مهرابانید. *mehrabāni/mehrabānid.* You are kind.

ما ترکیم. *mā torkim.* We are Turks.

جوانند. *javānand.* They are young.

اینها سیبند. *inhā siband.* These are apples.

دوستانم داخلند. *dustānam dāxeland.* My friends are inside.

After silent final ه (1/15), these forms are written
separately with initial *alef*:

تشنه‌ام. *tešne am.* I am thirsty.

خسته‌ایم. *xaste im.* We are tired.

After ا... *ā*, and و... *u/ou* we have the following joined
forms:

یم‍... -yam	ییم‍... -im
ی‍... -i	یید‍... -id
	یند‍... -yand

and after ـﻰ... -i the following joined forms:

م...	-am	یم...	-im
ی...	-i	ید...	-id
		ند...	-and

کجایند؟ *kojāyand?* Where are they?

جلویند. *jelouyand.* They are ahead.

دانشجویم. *dānešjūyam.* I am a student.

تبریزیم. *tabriziam.* I am a Tabrizi.

اصفهانیی\اصفهانیید؟ *esfahānii(d)?* Are you an Isfahani?

تنهایی\تنهایید. *tanhāi(d).* You are alone.

We also encounter these forms written separately with initial *alef*, but it is equally common to use the second form of the verb (see below) after any long vowel or vowel-combination (ا *ā,* و *u/ou,* ی *i/ei*).

- *The 3rd person singular form* (او\آن) is written as a separate word است *ast* when it follows a consonant or silent ه:

خوب است. *xub ast.* It is good.

ماشین بیرون است *mašin birun ast.* The car is outside.

در چرا باز است؟ *dar cerā bāz ast?*
Why is the door open?

خطش بسیار قشنگ است. *xatteš besyār qašang ast.*
His handwriting is very beautiful.

تازه است. *taze ast.* It is fresh.

این دونده خسته است *in davande xaste ast.*
This runner is tired.

برادرم نویسنده است. *barādaram nevisande ast.*
My brother is a writer.

بسته است. *baste ast.* It is closed.

In this form after a consonant (but not after silent ه), it has a colloquial pronunciation ‹e›:

خوب است. *xub* ‹e›. It's good.

After a long vowel ا *ā*, و *u* or ی *i* it usually drops its *alef* and becomes -*st*, joined to the word ending in the long vowel:

اینجاست. *injāst*. He is here.

مال اوست. *māle ust*. It is his.

ایرانیست. *irānist*. She is Iranian.

کیست؟ *kist?* Who is it?

Alternatively, it can be written separately with *alef* after و... -*u* or ی... -*i*. The pronunciation is the same, -*st*; after ی... the words may also be pronounced in full:

مال او است. *māle u st*.

ایرانی است. *irāni st/irāni ast*.

کی است؟ *kist/ki ast?*

After some words, the separated spelling is commoner:

او شخصی است که ... *u šaxsi st ke ...*
He is the person who ...

- The forms and endings *id/-id* and *and/-and* can be pronounced colloquially ‹*in*› and ‹*an*›.

Second form. This form consists only of complete words (i.e. no joined forms); it is very common. It is stressed on the syllable *hást*:

Persons	Singular		Plural	
1st	هستم	*hástam*	هستیم	*hástim*
2nd	هستی	*hásti*	هستید	*hástid* ‹*hástin*›
3rd	هست	*hast*	هستند	*hástand* ‹*hástan*›

Note:

- This form can be used instead of any of the first forms shown.
- This form is commonly used in preference to the first form other than است after a long vowel or vowel-combination:

دانشجو هستم. *dānešjū hastam*. I am a student.

تنها هستند. *tanhā hastand*. They are alone.

هندی هستی\هستید. *hendi hasti/hastid.* You are Indian.

جلو هستند. *jelou hastand.* They are ahead.

- This form is used when emphasis is needed on the verb:

ولی اینجا هستند. *vali injā hástand.* But they *are* here.

عرب هستند. *arab hástand.* They *are* Arab(s).

صحیح هست. *sahih hást.* It *is* true/correct.

- The 3rd person singular form هست *hast* also has the meaning 'there is', 'there are':

کار زیاد هست. *kāre ziyād hast.* There is a lot of work.

آیا ماشینها کافی هست؟ *āyā māšinhā kāfi hast?*
Are there enough cars?

چای هست؟ *cāi hast?* Is there any tea?

بله ، چای هست. – *bale, cāi hást.* - Yes, there *is* tea.

- *hastid* and *hastand* can be pronounced colloquially ‹*hastin*› and ‹*hastan*›.

Third form. This is regular (see 5/10), based on the present stem of بودن *budan* which is باش... *bāš-*:

می باشم *mí bāšam*	می باشیم *mí bāšim*
می باشی *mí bāši*	می باشید *mí bāšid*
می باشد *mí bāšad*	می باشند *mí bāšand*

(older spelling, still encountered: میباشم *míbāšam* [etc.], with joined prefix)

However spelt, this form of the verb is used only in official language, and should be avoided in ordinary writing or speaking. It is encountered in some public documents and reports, and heard in some formal speeches:

امروزه بیکاری بزرگترین مسئلۀ داخلی کشور می‌باشد.
emruze bikāri bozorgtarin masaleye dāxeliye kešvar mi bāšad.
Nowadays unemployment is the country's biggest internal problem.

Negative. The negative of 'to be' ('I am not ...') is:

نیستم *nístam*   نیستیم *nístim*
نیستی *nísti*   نیستید *nístid* ‹*nístin*›
نیست *nist*   نیستند *nístand* ‹*nístan*›

The stress is on the first syllable. *nistid* and *nistand* can be pronounced colloquially ‹*nistin*› and‹*nistan*› respectively. This is the only negative present-tense form of this verb in common use.

هنوز حاضر نیستیم. *hanuz hāzer nístim.* We're not ready yet.

اینطور نیست. *intour nist.* It isn't like that ('this').

مریض نیستم، خسته ام. *mariz nistam, xaste am.*
I'm not sick, I'm tired.

خوشحال نیستید؟ *xošhāl nistid?* Are you not happy?

کارگران راضی نیستند. *kārgarān rāzi nistand.*
The workmen are not satisfied.

12. Using the present tense

The present tense is used for any current or impending action or situation ('I do', 'I am doing', 'I shall/will do'):

نامه را می فهمم. *nāme rā mi fahmam.*
I understand the letter.

چه می گوید؟ *ce mi guyad?*
What does he say/is he saying?

حیف است که ... *heif ast ke ...* It is a pity that ...

عیب نیست. *eib nist.* It doesn't matter. ('It's no fault.')

معمولاً اینجا می نشینیم. *ma'mulan injā mi nešinim.*
We usually sit here.

چرا می خندید؟ *cerā mi xandid?*
Why are you laughing/do you laugh?

می بینید چرا ... *mi binid cerā ....* You (will) see why...

هفتۀ آینده می رسیم. *hafteye āyande mi rasim.*
We are arriving/shall arrive next week.

فردا به فرودگاه نمی روند. *fardā be forudgāh némi ravand.*
They are not going/will not go to the airport tomorrow.

A *future tense* exists for expressing a projected action or an expected situation; but it is used almost exclusively in written Persian or formal speech; it is examined in 5/27 and 28. In everyday Persian the present tense is used, as in the last example given above.

The present tense of certain verbs is also used for an action or situation which started previously and continues now. Such sentences often have a pattern corresponding to 'It is (so long) that ...':

- with بودن *budan* 'to be' in the affirmative:

سه سال است که اینجا هستم. *se sāl ast ke injā hastam.*
    I have been here (for) three years.
    ('It is three years that I am here').

چمد وقت اینطور است؟ *cand vaqt intour ‹e›?*
    How long has it been so?

- with verbs denoting an action (not a situation, except for بودن) in the affirmative:

سه سال است که این کرایه را می پردازم. *se sāl ast ke in kerāye rā mi pardāzam.* I have paid this rent for three years. ('It is three years that ...')

دو ساعت است که همین نامه را مینویسد. *do sā'at ast ke hamin nāme rā minevisad.*
He has been writing the same letter for two hours now.

This rule has exceptions and marginal cases. The sentence

او را چند سال می شناسم. *u rā cand sāl mi šenāsam.*
    I have known him for some years.

is logically not an action but a situation; yet it is better expressed with the present tense.

For such verbs denoting a *situation* (allowing for exceptions such as the one shown immediately above), and for the negative of all such verbs, we use the perfect tense, for which see 5/21, 22.

13. Forming the imperfect tense

The imperfect or continuous past tense ('I was doing', 'I used to do')

100

is formed with the

present prefix + past tense

See 5/10 and 8 above for these. The prefix is always stressed when the verb is affirmative. Two examples will suffice:

رفتن *raftan* to go (the stress is shown):

می رفتم *mí raftam*	می رفتیم *mí raftim*
می رفتی *mí rafti*	می رفتید *mí raftid*
می رفت *mí raft*	می رفتند *mí raftand*

I was going, I used to go (etc.)

خواندن *xāndan* to read:

می خواندم *mi xāndam*	می خواندیم *mi xāndim*
می خواندی *mi xāndi*	می خواندید *mi xāndid*
می خواند *mi xānd*	می خواندند *mi xāndand*

I was reading, I used to read (etc.)

The negative of this tense is formed exactly like the negative of the present tense, i.e. the prefix becomes نمی *némi* or *námi* :

نمی رفتم *némi raftam/námi raftam*
I was not going, I used not to go

نمی خواندم *némi xāndam/námi xāndam*
I was not reading, I used not to read

نمی آمد *némi āmad/námi āmad* (colloquially, ‹*némi umad*›)
he was not coming, he used not to come

This tense is not used for the verb بودن *budan* 'to be', or for داشتن *dāštan* 'to have' as a simple verb.

For the imperfect tense of *compound verbs*, see 5/29.

14. Using the imperfect tense

The imperfect or continuous past tense is used for a previous continuous or repeated action or situation which has now ceased:

آن وقت تاریخ می آموخت. *ān vaqt tārix mi āmuxt.*
At that time she was teaching history.

مرتباً به باشگاه می‌رفتند. *morattaban be bāšgāh mi raftand.*
They used to go regularly to the club.

همیشه پول خرد را دو بار می شمرد. *hamiše pule xord rā*
do bār mi šomord. He always counted the small change twice.

روزنامه را می‌خواندم که او رسید. *ruznāme rā mi xāndam ke u*
rasid/resid. I was reading the newspaper when he arrived.

The last example shows a continuous action (imperfect tense) interrupted by a single action (past tense). See 8/9.

There are two other important uses of the imperfect, explained elsewhere:

- In unreal conditions ('If I had known …' etc.), see 8/11.
- 'ought to have (done)', see 5/19 below.

15. Colloquial continuous tenses

Colloquial Persian has two continuous tenses. They are the colloquial present continuous and the colloquial past continuous. Each of these tenses consists respectively of the present or past tense (see 5/10 and 8) of داشتن دار... *daštan dār-* 'to have', followed by the present or imperfect tense (5/13) of the operative verb, both verbs in the pair agreeing with the subject. These tenses are sometimes also seen in writing, where dialogue is quoted.

From نوشتن نویس... *neveštan nevis-* to write:

Colloquial present continuous

دارم می نویسم ‹*dāram mi nevisam*›
داری می نویسی ‹*dāri mi nevisi*›
دارد می نویسد ‹*dāre mi nevise*›
داریم می نویسیم ‹*dārim mi nevisim*›
دارید می نویسید ‹*dārin mi nevisin*›
دارند می نویسند ‹*dāran mi nevisan*›

I'm writing, you're writing (etc.)

Colloquial past continuous

داشتم می نوشتم ‹dāštam mi neveštam›

داشتی می نوشتی ‹dāšti mi nevešti›

داشت می نوشت ‹dāšt mi nevešt›

داشتیم می نوشتیم ‹dāštim mi neveštim›

داشتید می نوشتید ‹dāštin mi neveštin›

داشتند می نوشتند ‹dāštan mi neveštan›

I was writing, you were writing (etc.)

The first verb of the pair usually follows its subject (or stands in place of its implied subject), the second verb standing at the end of the sentence or clause (see 8/4 for the definition of a clause):

رضا دارد روزنامه را می خواند. ‹rezā dāre ruznāme ro mi xune.› Reza's reading the newspaper.

داشتم لباس را می‌شستم ‹dāštam lebās ro mi šostam.› I was washing the clothes.

There is no negative form of these colloquial tenses.

See 5/29 for the use of these tenses with compound verbs.

16. Forming the present subjunctive tense

The present subjunctive tense (more conveniently called the 'subjunctive') expresses possibility or hypothesis ('I may do'). It is formed from the present tense (5/10 above) by replacing the present prefix می *mi* with the subjunctive prefix, which is always stressed, and always joined in writing. In the examples given below, verbs are indicated by their 'principal parts'.

Before present stems *beginning with a consonant*, the subjunctive prefix is ...بـ *bé*:

نوشتن نویس... *neveštan nevis-* to write (the stress is shown):

بنویسم *bénevisam*	بنویسیم *bénevisim*
بنویسی *bénevisi*	بنویسید *bénevisid*
بنویسد *bénevisad*	بنویسند *bénevisand*

I may write (etc.)

گفتن گو... *goftan gu-* to say:

بگویم *beguyam*	بگوییم *beguim*
بگویی *begui*	بگویید *beguid*
بگوید *beguyad*	بگویند *beguyand*

I may say (etc.)

Before present stems *beginning with a vowel other than i-,* the subjunctive prefix is ...بی *bí-.* In the combinations *bía-* and *bío-* the *alef* is dropped; in the combination *bíā-* the *madde* is dropped:

انداختن انداز... *andāxtan andāz-* to throw:

بیندازم ، بیندازی ... *biandāzam, biandāzi* (etc.)
I may throw (etc.)

افتادن افت... *oftādan oft-* to fall:

بیفتم ، بیفتی ... *bioftam, biofti* (etc.) I may fall (etc.)

آمدن آ... *āmadan ā-* to come:

بیایم ، بیایی ... *biāyam, biāi* (etc.) I may come (etc.)

Before the only present stem *beginning with i-,* the prefix is ...ب *bé-* and the *alef* of the verb is kept:

ایستادن ایست... *istādan ist-* to stand, to stop:

بایستم ، بایستی ... *béistam, béisti* (etc.) I may stand, stop (etc.)

With verbs having a vowel *u* or *o* in the present stem, the subjunctive prefix may also be pronounced *bó-* (the stress being maintained). Examples:

کردن کن... *kardan kon-* to do:

بکنم ، بکنی ... *bókonam, bókoni* (etc.) I may do (etc.)

خوردن خور... *xordan xor-* to eat, to drink:

بخورم ، بخوری ... *boxoram, boxori* (etc.) I may eat/drink (etc.)

گفتن گو... *goftan gu-* to say:

بگویم ، بگویی ... *boguyam, bogui* (etc.) I may say (etc.)

گذاشتن گذار... *gozāštan gozār-* to put:

بگذارم ، بگذاری ... *bogozāram, bogozāri* (etc.)
I may put (etc.)

The subjunctive of ...بودن باش budan bāš- 'to be' is formed with

present stem + personal ending (i.e. no prefix)

The stress is on the first syllable:

...بودن باش budan bāš- to be (the stress is shown):

باشم	bā́šam	باشيم	bā́šim
باشی	bā́ši	باشيد	bā́šid
باشد	bā́šad	باشند	bā́šand

I may be (etc.)

The present subjunctive tense of ...داشتن دار dāštan dār- 'to have' is little used; instead we use the *perfect subjunctive* tense, for which see 5/23.

Colloquial pronunciation. The elements of colloquial pronunciation (see 2/6) found in the present tense apply also to the subjunctive:

...ماندن مان mā́ndan mān-/‹mun-› to remain:

‹bémunam, bémuni, bémune; bémunim, bémunin, bémunan›

...شدن شو šodan šav-/‹š-› to become:

‹bešam, beši, beše; bešim, bešin, bešan›

...بودن باش budan bāš- to be:

‹bāšam, bāši, bāše; bāšim, bāšin, bāšan›

In ...آمدن آ āmadan ā- 'to come'; -āya- becomes -ā-:

‹biām, biāi, biād; biāim, biāin, biān›

The alternative pronunciation *bo-* of the prefix for certain verbs (see above) is not used when the colloquial present stem has no vowel *u* or *o*. For e.g. ...گفتن گو goftan gu-/‹g-› and ...گذاشتن گذار gozāštan gozār-/‹zār-› we have:

‹bégam, bégi, bége; bégim, bégin, bégan›

‹bezāram, bezāri, bezāre; bezārim, bezārin, bezāran›

Negative. The negative subjunctive ('I may not do') is made by dropping the ...بیـ\...بـ bé-/bí- prefix of the affirmative form, and substituting the negative prefix ...نـ ná-. The negative prefix then

105

takes the stress of the word:

نكنم *nákonam* I may not do   نگوییم *náguim* we may not say

نرود *náravad* he may not go   ننویسند *nánevisand*
they may not write

Before a vowel, this prefix follows exactly the same pattern as that shown for the negative past tense (see 5/8):

نیاید *náyāyad* he may not come   نیفتد *náyoftad* it may not fall

نیاورم *náyāvaram* I may not bring   نایستند *náistand*
they may not stop

For the negative subjunctive of بودن باش... *budan bāš-* 'to be' we attach the stressed negative prefix directly to the affirmative form:

نباشم، نباشی ... *nábāšam, nábāši* (etc.) I may not be (etc.).

For the present subjunctive tense of *compound verbs*, see 5/29.

17. Using the present subjunctive tense

The present subjunctive tense expresses possibility rather than fact. It has three principal uses:

- to express the imperative for certain persons; see 5/18 below.

- after certain auxiliary verbs, examined in 5/19:

باید بروم *bāyad beravam* I must go

نمی خواهد بیاید. *nemi xāhad biāyad.*
He does not want to come.

- after certain conjunctions, to express probability, anticipation, purpose and the like, examined in 8/5, 6, 7, 9, 11:

زود بروید تا سر وقت برسید. *zud beravid tā sare vaqt berasid.* Go quickly so that you arrive on time.

اگر امروز برسد ... *agar emruz berasad ...*
If he/she arrives today ...

18. Imperative

The imperative or command form of the verb is derived from the present subjunctive tense (the 'subjunctive'), for which see 5/16 above.

For the 1st and 3rd persons (singular and plural), the form is identical to the subjunctive (affirmative or negative), which then has the meaning 'let me (etc.) do/not do':

گفتن گو... *goftan gu-* to say (the stress is shown):

بگویم *béguyam* let me say   بگوییم *béguim* let us say

بگوید *béguyad* let him/her say   نگویند *náguyand* let them not say

When put into a question, these forms have the meaning 'should I (etc.) (not) do?' or 'may I (etc.) (not) do?':

چه بگویم؟ *ce beguyam ‹begam›?* What should I say?

فردا نیایند؟ *fardā nayāyand ‹nayānd›?* May they not/Should they not come tomorrow?

احمد هم برود؟ *ahmad ham beravad ‹bere›?* Should Ahmad go too?

For the 2nd persons, the form is identical to the subjunctive *minus final* ی\یی... -*i* in the singular (تو), and identical to the unchanged subjunctive in the plural (شما). The meaning is that of a direct command, 'Do/Do not':

بنویس *bénevis* write   ننویسید *nánevisid* do not write

بیا\بیایید *biā(id)* come   نیا\نیایید *naya(id)* do not come

بکشید *bekašid* pull   نکشید *nakašid* don't pull

بپرسید *beporsid* ask   نپرسید *naporsid* don't ask

The imperative of بودن باش... *budan bāš-* 'to be' follows the rules given above. Like the subjunctive, it has no prefix in the affirmative:

خاطر جمع باشید. *xāter jam' bāšid.* Be (re)assured.

دلتنگ نباش. *deltang nábāš.* Don't be downhearted.

For verbs whose present stem has *the vowel o*, the prefix ...بـ is pronounced *bo-*:

بکن\بکنید *bokon(id)* Do

هم اینجا بگذارند. *ham injā bogozārand.*
Let them put (it) just here.

چای را بخور.* *cāi rā boxor.* Drink (your) tea.

* و is silent here, see 1/13.

For verbs whose present stem has *the vowel u written with* و , the prefix ...بـ may be pronounced either *be-* or *bo*:

بگو\بگویید *begu(id)/bogu(id)* Say, Tell

For verbs whose present stem has *the sound av written* و , then in *the 2nd person singular only* (تو) this syllable is pronounced *ou*, and the prefix ...بـ may be pronounced either *be-* or *bo*:

برو\نرو *berou (borou)/narou* Go/Don't go (singular)

but: بروید\نروید *beravid/naravid* Go/Don't go (plural)

The imperative of the simple verb داشتن دار... *dāštan dār-* 'to have' is little used; if an imperative is needed it is derived from the perfect subjunctive tense: داشته باشید *dāšte bāšid* 'have' (etc.). See 5/23.

Perhaps the most frequently used imperative is بفرمایید *befarmāid*, used when offering or proposing something (see 12/6). It is the equivalent of German 'Bitte' or Italian 'Prego'. Used in this sense, this word is always plural and affirmative:

بفرمایید. *befarmāid.*
Please do/go ahead/help yourself.

از این طرف بفرمایید خانم. *az in taraf befarmāid xānom.*
Come this way, ma'am.

سؤال هست؟ بفرمایید. *so'āl hast? befarmāid.*
Are there questions? Please (ask).

Colloquial pronunciation. Colloquial pronunciation (see 2/6) applies to the imperative exactly as it does to the subjunctive:

برویم. ‹bérim›. Let's go.

اینجا بیایید. injā ‹bíain›. Come here.

الآن بیایند. ‹alon bíānd› Let them come now.

For the imperative of *compound verbs*, see 5/29.

19. Auxiliary verbs

An auxiliary verb is a verb used in combination with another verb. The auxiliary expresses such ideas as capability, volition, obligation with relation to the second verb. Typical English auxiliary expressions (with the auxiliary underlined) are 'I can come', 'he wants to go', 'we must write'. In English the second or operative verb stands in the *infinitive*; in Persian it stands in a tense, (mostly the *present subjunctive*, 5/16 above), in the same person as the auxiliary verb.

The auxiliary verb usually stands immediately after its subject (or in the place of its implied subject); the subjunctive verb stands at the end of the sentence or clause (see 8/4). Where appropriate, the auxiliaries are shown below with their principal parts (5/10 above).

The important auxiliary verbs are:

توانستن توانـ... *tavānestan tavān-* can, to be able

بایستن *bāyestan* must, to have to

خواستن خواهـ... *xāstan xāh-* to want

شاید *šāyad* may (perhaps)

They are used as follows:

- توانستن توانـ... *tavānestan tavān-* can, to be able. The present tense of this verb is formed in the usual way, see 5/10 above. Its present stem has a colloquial pronunciation (see 2/6) ‹tun-›:

می‌تواند فردا برود. *mi tavānad fardā beravad.*
‹mi tune fardā bere› He can go tomorrow.

نمی توانم خوب بفهمم. *nemi tavānam ‹nemi tunam›*
xub befahmam. I cannot understand properly ('well').

آیا همکارتان می تواند این صندوق را بالا بگذارد؟
āyā hamkāretān mi tavānad in sanduq rā bālā begozārad?
Can your colleague put this box upstairs?

از این پنجره می توانم مسجد را ببینم.
az in panjare mi tavānam masjed rā bebinam.
From this window I can see the mosque.

چرا نمی توانند جواب را بفرستند؟ *cerā nemi tavānand*
javāb rā beferestand? Why can they not send the answer?

هیچکس نمی تواند این خطّ را بخواند.
hickas nemi tavānad in xat rā bexānad.
Nobody can read this handwriting.

For past meaning, the imperfect (5/13 above) of this verb is the most commonly used tense. In this verb the *past stem* also has a colloquial pronunciation, *‹tunest-›*:

می توانستند دو تا بخرند. *mi tavānestand do tā bexarand.*
‹mi tunestand› ... They were able to buy two.

نمی توانستیم بیاییم. *nemi tavānestim ‹nemi tunestim›*
biāim. We couldn't come/we were unable to come.

The simple past tense (5/8 above) is used mostly in the negative, with the implied meaning 'tried but failed':

پروین نتوانست در را خوب ببندد.
parvin natavānest dar rā xub bebandad.
Parvin was unable to close the door properly.

از صدای هواپیماها نتوانستم بخوابم. *az sedāye*
havāpeimāhā natavānestam ‹natunestam› bexābam.
I couldn't sleep for the noise of the aeroplanes.

- بایستن *bāyestan* must, to have (to). This verb is defective, having only one present form and one past form, used for all persons. The verb following it agrees with the subject as usual.

باید *bāyad* 'must'; (present form) is used:

- with the present subjunctive, 'must', 'have to/has to':

باید با دقت بشماریم. *bāyad ba deqqat bešomārim.*
We must count accurately.

نباید غذا را تند تند بخوری. *nabāyad qazā ra*
tond tond boxori. You mustn't eat (your) food (so) fast.

باید این حساب را امروز بپردازم. *bāyad in hesāb rā*
emruz bepardāzam. I must pay this bill today.

نباید اینطور بگویید. *nabāyad intour beguid.*
You must not say that ('thus').

بچه‌ها باید توی خیابان مواظب باشند.
baccehā bāyad tuye xiābān movāzeb bāšand.
Children have to be careful on ('in') the street.

هر دانشجو باید دفتری بیاورد. *har dānešju bāyad*
daftari biāvarad. Every student has to bring a notebook.

- with the perfect subjunctive (5/23, 24 below), 'must
have (done)', 'presumably has/have (done)':

رضا باید دیر رسیده باشد. *rezā bāyad dir raside*
bāšad. Reza must (presumably) have arrived late.

باید منزل مانده باشند. *bāyad manzel mānde bāšand.*
They must have stayed at home.

پروین باید این نامه را نوشته باشد.
parvin bāyad in nāme rā nevešte bāšad.
Parvin must have written this letter.

بایست *bāyest* (past form) is used:

- with the present subjunctive, 'ought to':

بایست راست بگویی. *bāyest rāst begui.*
You ought to tell the truth.

بایست مواظب باشند. *bāyest movāzeb bāšand.*
They ought to be careful.

نباست اینطور بکنیم. *nabāyest intour bokonim.*
We ought not to do that ('thus').

- with the imperfect tense (5/13 above), 'ought to/should
have (done)':

بایست زودتر می آمدید. *bāyest zudtar mi āmadid.*
You ought to/should have come sooner (but didn't).

111

بچه ها بایست منزل می ماندند.

baccehā bāyest manzel mi māndand.

The children should have stayed (at) home.

'had to', which is in English the past corresponding to 'must', is best expressed indirectly in Persian also. The easiest formula is مجبور بودن *majbur budan* 'to be forced', with the dependent verb in the present subjunctive:

مجبور بودیم اضافه بپردازیم. *majbur budim ezāfe*

bepardāzim. We had to ('were forced to') pay extra.

There is no different colloquial pronunciation for باید or بایست.

- خواستن خواه... *xāstan xāh-* (silent و, see 1/13) to want. The tenses are formed regularly. Present-tense examples:

می‌خواهند امروز بیایند. *mi xāhand emruz biāyand.*

They want to come today.

می‌خواهم یك كوزه و چند تا كاسه بخرم. *mi xāham yek kuze o cand tā kāse bexaram.*

I want to buy a jug and some bowls.

می‌خواهند خانه را بفروشند. *mi xāhand xāne rā*

beforušand. They want to sell the house.

كی می‌خواهد اینجا بنشیند؟ *ki mi xāhad injā benešinad?*

Who wants to sit here?

بیشتر نمی‌خواهم بمانم. *bištar nemi xāham bemānam.*

I don't want to stay any longer ('more').

For past meaning ('wanted'), the imperfect of this verb is the most commonly used form:

می‌خواستم نامه بنویسم. *mi xāstam nāme benevisam.*

I wanted to write a letter.

می‌خواستند تاكسی بگیرند. *mi xāstand tāksi begirand.*

They wanted to take/get a taxi.

رضا نمی‌خواست بماند. *rezā nemi xāst bemānad.*

Reza didn't want to stay.

The simple past tense expresses 'was/were about to':

خواستم بروم. *xāstam beravam.* I was about to go.

112

The verb خواستن also translates 'to ask for' (with از *az* before the person asked). Both in this meaning and in the meaning 'to want', it can take a direct object:

از صندوقدار مساعده خواست. *az sanduqdār mosā'ede xāst.* He asked the cashier for an advance.

کارگرها اضافه می‌خواهند. *kārgarhā ezāfe mi xāhand.* The workmen want/are asking for a rise.

In the colloquial pronunciation of the present stem of this verb, *-āha-* becomes *-ā*:

‹*mi xām, mi xāhi, mi xād; mi xāhim, mi xāhin, mi xān*›

• شاید *šāyad* may (perhaps). Like بایستن *bāyestan*, the verb شایستن *šāyestan* is defective. It has only an invariable present شاید *šāyad* 'may'. In literary Persian this verb counts as an auxiliary and is followed by the subjunctive; but in everyday Persian شاید is very commonly used simply as an adverb meaning 'perhaps', with the operative verb in an appropriate non-subjunctive tense:

شاید فردا برود. *šāyad fardā beravad.* She may (perhaps) go tomorrow.

شاید همه اش را بدانند\می دانند. *šāyad hamaš rā bedānand/ mi dānand.* Perhaps they know everything.

For the negative, we negate the dependent verb, not the auxiliary:

شاید نرود\نمی‌رود. *šāyad naravad/nemi ravad.* She may (probably) not go.

شاید هیچ چیز نگفت. *šāyad hic ciz nagoft.* Perhaps he said nothing.

There is no different colloquial pronunciation for this auxiliary verb.

Impersonal expressions. Three auxiliary verbs, two of them described above, are used with the *short infinitive* (5/2 above) to make impersonal expressions ('one can do' etc.):

- 'one can', 'one could'. For this we have two formulæ:

  - the form می توان *mi tavān* (present) + short infinitive, in which the auxiliary has no personal ending:

  از اینجا مسجد را می توان دید. *az injā masjed rā mi tavān did.* You ('One') can see the mosque from here.

  نمی توان آنطور گفت. *nemi tavān āntour goft.* One cannot say that ('thus').

  The present stem *tavān-* is not usually pronounced colloquially in this usage.

  - the 3rd person singular (او\آن) form می شود *mi šavad* (present) or می شد *mi šod* (imperfect) of شدن شو... *šodan šav-* 'to become' + short infinitive. This is especially common in speech, and colloquial pronunciation may be used:

  می شود اینطور گفت؟ *mi šavad/‹mi še› intour goft?* Can you say this ('thus')?

  – نه نمی شود. *– na, ‹nemi še›.* - No, you can't.

  نمی شد خوب شنید. *nemi šod xub šenid.* One could not hear well.

- 'one must', 'one ought to'. For these, we use the already impersonal forms باید *bāyad* (present) or بایست *bāyest* (past), + short infinitive:

  باید همیشه راست گفت. *bāyad hamiše rāst goft.* One must always tell the truth.

  نباید مأیوس شد. *nabāyad ma'yus šod.* One must not lose hope ('become desperate').

  بایست زود تصمیم گرفت. *bāyest zud tasmim gereft.* One ought to take a decision quickly.

See 5/29 for the use of auxiliary verbs with *compound verbs*.

اصفهان، میدان امام (میدان شاه)

esfahān - meidāne emām (meidāne šāh)
Isfahan - Imam Square (King's Square)

20. Participles

Participles are adjectives derived from verbs. Like English, Persian has two participles: the *present participle* ('doing') and the *past participle* ('done').

Present participle. This participle is formed by adding to the present stem (5/10 above) the ending نده... *-andé* (after a vowel, ینده... *-yandé*; both forms with silent final ه , see 1/15). The participle is stressed on its last vowel:

Present stem	Present participle
نویس... *nevis-* write	نویسنده *nevisandé* writing
فروش... *foruš-* sell	فروشنده *forušandé* selling
آ... *ā-* come	آینده *āyandé* coming

Past participle. This participle is formed by adding to the past stem (5/8 above) the stressed ending *-é* (with silent ه):

Past stem	Past participle
رسید... *rasid-/resid-* arrived	رسیده *rasidé/residé* arrived

115

کرد... ‍ *kard-* did   کرده ‍ *kardé* done

گذشت... ‍ *gozašt-* passed   گذشته ‍ *gozašté* passed

نوشت... ‍ *nevešt-* wrote   نوشته ‍ *nevešté* written

Use of the present participle. The *present participle* is in principle a verbal adjective, but its use as such is very limited. Often the participle is best translated by a non-verbal adjective in English:

سال آینده ‍ *sāle āyande* next year

نسلهای آینده ‍ *naslhāye āyande* future generations

More common is the use of this participle as a noun, denoting the person or thing performing the action of the verb:

فروشنده ‍ *forušande* vendor, salesman/woman

نماینده ‍ *namāyande* representative

نویسنده ‍ *nevisande* writer

آینده ‍ *āyande* the future

There are two uses of the English '-ing' verbal form which are *not* expressed with the Persian present participle:

- the English continuous tenses ('I am doing', 'I was doing'), for which Persian uses the present (5/10) or imperfect (5/13) tenses, or one of the colloquial continuous tenses (5/15),
- the English verbal noun, e.g. 'reading', for which Persian uses the long infinitive, 5/2 above.

Not all theoretically possible present participles are in use.

Use of the past participle. The *past participle* is used as an adjective in certain cases; sometimes, like the present participle, it is best translated with a non-verbal adjective in English:

بانک بسته است. ‍ *bānk baste ast.* The bank is closed.

پنجرهٔ شکسته‌ای ‍ *panjareye šekastei* a broken window

ماه گذشته ‍ *māhe gozašte* last month, the past month

سیب رسیده ‍ *sibe raside* the ripe apple/ripe apples*

(* singular collective noun, see 3/4.)

A second use is as a noun:

گذشته gozašte the past

نوشته‌ها neveštehā writings, written works

A third use is in a verbal phrase, 'having (done)':

اینطور گفته، بلند شد و رفت. intour gofte, boland šod o raft.

Having said that ('thus'), she stood up and left ('went').

The past participle is also used in two verb forms:

- in the *perfect*, *perfect subjunctive* and *pluperfect* tenses, for which see 5/21, 23 and 25,
- in the *passive voice*, for which see 5/30.

The past participle can be made negative in the same manner as the past tense:

نگفته nágofte not (having) said

A negative present participle exists in theory but is extremely rare.

See 3/4 for literary plurals of nouns ending in silent ه, which include both types of participles, e.g. نمایندگان namāyandegān 'representatives', نوشته جات\نوشتجات neveštejāt 'writings'.

See 7/6 for adverbial participles, less common than adjectival participles.

21. Forming the perfect tense

The perfect tense ('I have done') is formed with

past participle + first form of 'to be' (present)

See 5/20 and 11 respectively for these. In the perfect tense the form of 'to be' follows silent ه, and is therefore written separately, with initial *alef* (see 5/11, first and second indents).

زود رسیده ایم. zud rasidé im. We have arrived early.

او هم رفته است. u ham rafté ast. He has gone too.

بچه‌ها این را نوشته اند. baccehā in rā nevešté and.

The children have written this.

In the affirmative tense the stress is on the final vowel of the participle.

For the negative of this tense, we negate the participle. The stress
shifts on to the prefix:

هنوز نرسیده است. *hanuz náraside ast.* He has not yet arrived.

نیامده اند؟ *náyāmade and?* Have they not come?

هیچ نامه ننوشته ایم. *hic náme nánevešte im.*
We have written no letter/We have not written any letter.

For the perfect tense of *compound verbs*, see 5/29.

22. Using the perfect tense

The perfect tense is used, as in English, for a previous action or
situation whose effect is still felt now:

رسیده اند. *raside and.* They have arrived (and are still here).

رئیس فرموده است که ... *rais farmude ast ke ...*
The director has ordered that ...

In everyday speech, the elements است *ast* and اند *and* are often
omitted:

ماشین نیامده؟ *māšin ‹nayumade›?* Hasn't the car come?

– چرا آمده. *– cerā, ‹umade›.* –Yes, it has.

همهٔ مهمانها رفته. *hameye mehmānhā rafte.*
All the guests have gone.

Just as the present tense can convey future meaning (5/12), so the
perfect tense can convey a future-perfect meaning ('I shall/will have
done') when appropriate:

تا آن موقع ما رفته ایم. *tā ān mouqe' mā rafte im.*
By then we (shall) have gone.

The perfect tense is not normally used for a previous action having
no effect on the present situation; that requires either the past
tense (5/8, 9) or the imperfect tense (5/13, 14).

For a previous action or situation which *itself* continues into the
present, Persian uses either the perfect or the present tense (5/10,
11, 12), as follows:

- When the verb (whether denoting action or situation) is

negative, the perfect is used:

از آن وقت بیرون نرفته است. *az ān vaqt birun narafte
ast.* Since then he/she has not gone out.

دو ماه حقوق نپرداخته اند. *do māh hoquq napardāxte
and.* They have paid no salary for two months.

ایشان را از دیروز ندیده ام. *išān rā az diruz nadide am.*
I have not seen him/her/them since yesterday.

هیچوقت آنطور نبوده است. *hicvaqt āntour nabude ast.*
It has never been so.

* For a verb other than بودن *budan* 'to be' denoting a situation
  in the affirmative, the perfect is used:

شاهدان نیم ساعت نشسته اند. *šāhedān nim sā'at nešaste
and.* The witnesses have been sitting for half an hour.

از تابستان مانده اند. *az tābestān mānde and.*
They have been staying since the summer.

* For بودن *budan* 'to be' in the affirmative, or for a verb
  denoting an action in the affirmative, we use the present
  tense; see 5/12.

An ambiguity arises when certain past participles are used as
adjectives with the present tense of بودن *budan*; this structure
looks like the perfect tense but should not be confused with it:

پنجره شکسته است. *panjare šekaste ast.*
The window is broken.

جمعه ها بانکها بسته اند. *jom'ehā bānkhā baste and.*
On Friday ('Fridays') the banks are closed.

This use is confined to verbs which can take a direct object (see
5/6). With sentences such as these the ambiguity can be avoided
by using the second form of بودن *budan* (see 5/11):

جمعه ها بانکها بسته هستند. *jom'ehā bānkhā baste hastand.*

23. Forming the perfect subjunctive tense

The perfect subjunctive tense ('(that) I might do', '(that) I may have
done') is formed with

119

<u>past participle + subjunctive of بودن *budan* 'to be'</u>

(See 5/20 and 16 respectively for these.)

کرده باشم *kardé bāšam* (that) I might do

نوشته باشد *nevešté bāšad* (that) he/she might write

خوانده باشیم *xāndé bāšim* (that) we might read

When the verb is affirmative the stress of the whole tense lies on the final vowel of the participle.

The negative of this tense is formed by making the participle negative. The stress shifts on to the negative prefix, as always:

نرفته\نیامده باشد *nárafte/náyāmade bāšad*
(that) he might not go/come

ندیده باشید *nádide bāšid* (that) you might not see

نگرفته باشند *nágerefte bāšand* (that) they might not take

The perfect subjunctive tense of داشتن دار... *daštan dār-* 'to have' is used instead of the subjunctive tense. It mostly therefore has present, not perfect, meaning:

داشته باشم *dāšte bāšam*   داشته باشیم *dāšte bāšim*

داشته باشی *dāšte bāši*   داشته باشید *dāšte bāšid*

داشته باشد *dāšte bāšad*   داشته باشند *dāšte bāšand*

(that) I may have (etc.)

Negative: ... نداشته باشم *nádāšte bāšam* (etc.)

This gives us the imperative (see 5/18) of داشتن, which is identical to the perfect subjunctive except for the 2nd person singular (تو) form, (نـ)داشته باش *(ná)dāšte bāš* '(don't) have'.

These are the subjunctive tense and imperative forms used when this verb is used as a simple verb (5/5 above). Its simple imperative is rarely used. The forms are different, and more common in use, when this verb occurs as the verbal element of a compound verb.

For the perfect subjunctive tense of *compound verbs*, see 5/29.

24. Using the perfect subjunctive tense

The perfect subjunctive tense expresses possibility rather than fact.

The perfect subjunctive of داشتن دار... *daštan dār-* 'to have' is used instead of the present subjunctive, e.g. after an auxiliary verb (5/19 above):

باید وقت زیاد داشته باشیم. *bāyad vaqte ziād dāšte bāšim.*
We have to have a lot of time.

هر سرباز باید نمره ای داشته باشد. *har sarbāz bāyad nomrei dāšte bāšad.* Every soldier must have a number.

and for the imperative of certain persons, see 5/23.

Two other important uses of the perfect subjunctive (of all verbs, including داشتن *daštan*) are explained elsewhere:

- after certain conjunctions, to express a probability, hope, purpose and the like (8/5, 7, 9, 11):

  می ترسم که آنها هم رفته باشند. *mi tarsam ke ānhā ham rafte bāšand.* I fear they (may) have gone too.

- with the auxiliary verb باید *bāyad*, to express 'must have (done)', 'presumably has/have (done)', see 5/19.

The perfect subjunctive tense of بودن باش... *budan bāš-* 'to be' is rarely used.

25. Forming the pluperfect tense

The pluperfect tense ('I had done') is formed with

past participle + past tense of بودن *budan* 'to be'

(See 5/20 and 5/8 respectively for these.)

When affirmative, the verb is stressed on the final vowel of the participle:

نوشته بودم *nevešté budam* I had written

The negative of this tense is formed by making the participle negative. The stress then moves back to the prefix:

نبرده\نیاورده بود *náborde/náyāvorde bud*
she had not taken/brought

For the pluperfect tense of *compound verbs*, see 5/29.

26. Using the pluperfect tense

The pluperfect tense denotes a completed action or state situated
farther back in time than the past tense (5/8 above), or one which
preceded another completed action or state:

چند وقت پیش رسیده بودیم. *cand vaqte piš raside budim.*
We had arrived some time before.

هنوز ننشسته بودم که پیانیست شروع کرد.
hanuz nanešaste budam ke piānist šoru' kard.
I had hardly ('not yet') sat down when the pianist began.

Some ambiguity arises when certain past participles are used as
adjectives with the past tense of بودن *budan*; this structure looks
like the pluperfect tense but should not be confused with it:

دکان بسته بود. *dokkān baste bud.* The shop was closed.

This use is confined to verbs which can take a direct object (see
5/6).

The pluperfect of ...بودن باش *budan bāš-* 'to be' is not used.

27. Forming the future tense

The future tense ('I shall do') is formed with

auxiliary verb + short infinitive

The auxiliary verb in question is خواستن خواه... *xāstan xāh-* 'to
want' (5/19) in the present tense, *minus its present prefix*, thus:

خواهم، خواهی، خواهد؛ خواهیم، خواهید، خواهند
xāham, xāhi, xāhad; xāhim, xāhid, xāhand

See 5/2 for the short infinitive.

There is no different colloquial pronunciation for the auxiliary verb
in this use.

For the negative of this tense we prefix ...نـ *ná-* to the auxiliary.

The stress of the whole tense is on the auxiliary - on its *personal ending* (NB) in the affirmative, on its prefix in the negative:

خواهم نوشت *xahám nevešt* I shall write

نخواهم نوشت *náxaham nevešt* I shall not write

آسان خواهد بود. *asan xahád bud*. It will be easy.

آسان نخواهد بود. *asan náxahad bud*. It will not be easy.

The auxiliary and the short infinitive almost always stay together, at the end of the clause or sentence (see 8/4 for the definition of a clause).

28. Using the future tense

The future tense denotes an action or state clearly situated ahead of the present. It is used mostly in writing, and then to denote an intention, or to emphasise the future timing of the verb, or when no other expression in the sentence makes the future timing clear:

جواب شدیدی خواهیم نوشت. *javabe šadidi xahim nevešt.*
We shall write a stern reply.

سخت است ولی آسانتر خواهد شد. *saxt ast vali asantar xahad šod.* It is difficult but it will get ('become') easier.

When the future timing is clear from the context, or the action is imminent, the present tense with future meaning (5/12 above) is commonly used instead:

فردا می‌آیند. *farda mi ayand.*
They are coming (= will come) tomorrow.

The future tense is also commonly used (also in speech) to express a supposition, as in English:

کی این را نوشته است؟ - عباس خواهد بود.
ki in ra nevešte ast? - abbas xahad bud.
Who's written this? It'll be/I presume it's Abbas.

For the future tense of *compound verbs*, see 5/29 below.

29. Compound verbs

See 5/5. Persian has relatively few simple verbs; for any but the most basic concepts a compound verb is used. The compound consists of a non-verbal element and a simple verb. The verbs quoted below are only a small sample; they are shown with the principal parts (5/10 above) of their verbal element:

باز کردن کنـ... *bāz kardan kon-* to open

تلفن کردن کنـ... *telefon kardan kon-* to telephone

کار کردن کنـ... *kār kardan kon-* to work, to do

کوشش کردن کنـ... *kušeš kardan kon-* to try

زندگی کردن کنـ... *zendegi kardan kon-* to live

کمك کردن کنـ... *komak kardan kon-* to help

بر خاستن خیز... *bar xāstan xiz-* to rise

بر گشتن گرد.... *bar gaštan gard-* to return

پیش آمدن آ... *piš āmadan ā-* to occur

وارد شدن شو... *vāred šodan šav-* to enter

میل داشتن دار... *meil dāštan dār-* to like, to want

دوست داشتن دار.... *dust dāštan dār-* to like

جرأت داشتن دار.... *jor'at dāštan dār-* to dare

بر داشتن دار.... *bar dāštan dār-* to remove

جواب دادن دهـ.. *javāb dādan deh-* to answer

درس دادن دهـ... *dars dādan deh-* to teach

درس خواندن خوانـ... *dars xāndan xān-* to study

زحمت کشیدن کشـ... *zahmat kašidan kaš-* to take trouble

طول کشیدن کشـ... *tul kašidan kaš-* to last

زنگ زدت زنـ... *zang zadan zan-* to ring

زمین خوردن خور... *zamin xordan xor-* to fall

The non-verbal element may in some cases be a phrase beginning with a preposition (see 6/2):

به هم خوردن خور... *be hám xordan xor-* to fall apart

از بین رفتن رو... *az beín raftan rav-* to disappear

به کار بردن برـ... *be kār bordan bar-* to use

For the most part, the two elements of the compound verb stay together, at the end of the sentence or clause (see 8/4 for the definition of a clause):

از بین نمی رود. *az bein nemi ravad.*
It does not go away.

مرتباً پیش می آمد. *morattaban piš mi āmad.*
It occurred regularly.

به او کمك نمی کردند. *be u komak nemi kardand.*
They did not help her.

کوشش نکرده است. *kušeš nakarde ast.* He has not tried.

دو سال طول نخواهد کشید. *do sāl tul naxāhad kašid.*
It will not last two years.

Any direct-object pronoun suffix م... -*am*, ت... -*et*/-*at* (etc., see 4/3) is added to the non-verbal element:

بازش نکن. *bāzeš nakon.* Don't open it.

خیلی دوستش داریم. *xeili dusteš dārim.* We like it a lot.

With some compound verbs having a noun as non-verbal element, the compound may be interrupted by anything needed to complete the meaning, such as:

- an *ezāfe* (3/5, 8) + noun, pronoun, or adjective, with or without a direct-object suffix را *rā* (3/3), following the noun of the compound,
- a plural suffix (3/4), the indefinite suffix ی...-*i* (3/2) and/or the direct-object suffix را *rā* following the noun of the compound.

جرأت شکایت نداشتم. *jor'ate šekāyat nadāštam.*
I didn't dare (to) complain.

جواب نامه را ندادند. *javābe nāme rā nadādand.*
They did not answer the letter.

امروز درس خیلی آسانی را داد. *emruz darse xeili āsāni rā dād.*
Today he taught a very easy lesson.

کدام درسها را می خوانیم؟ *kodam daršhā rā mi xānim?*
Which lessons are we studying?

125

زحمت زیاد کشیده است؟ راستی؟ چه زحمتی کشیده است؟

zahmate ziād kašide ast? rāsti? ce zahmati kašide ast?

He has taken a lot of trouble? Really? What trouble has he taken?

With a few verbs, an *ezāfe* can also be added to the non-verbal element where this is other than a noun:

کشتی وارد بندر شد. *kašti vārede bandar šod.* The ship entered the harbour. (وارد *vāred*, adjective, 'entering')

Tenses and parts. In all tenses and parts, the compound verb is stressed in the affirmative on its non-verbal element, and in the negative on the negative prefix. While the non-verbal element of the compound verb remains unchanged, the verbal element forms its tenses and other parts in the usual manner, with the exception of the subjunctive tense and imperative:

- Infinitives. Long and short infinitives (5/2 above):

پیدا کردن\کرد *peidā kardan/kard* to find

- Stems, tenses, participles. Past and present stems and tenses (5/8, 10, 11), imperfect tense (5/13), present and past participles (5/20), perfect (5/21), perfect subjunctive (5/23), pluperfect (5/25) and future tenses (5/27):

یاد گرفتن گیر... *yād gereftan gir-* to learn:

یاد (نـ)گرفتم *yād (na)gereftam*
I learnt/did not learn

یاد (نـ)می‌گیرم *yād (ne)mi giram* I (do not) learn

یاد (نـ)می‌گرفتم *yād (ne)mi gereftam*
I was (not) learning

یاد گیرنده *yād girande* learning

یاد گرفته *yād gerefte* learnt

یاد (نـ)گرفته ام *yād (na)gerefte am*
I have (not) learnt

یاد (نـ)گرفته باشم *yād (na)gerefte bāšam*
I might (not) learn

یاد (نـ)گرفته بودم *yād (na)gerefte budam*
I had (not) learn

126

یاد (نـ)خواهم گرفت *yād (na)xāham gereft*
I shall (not) learn

- Subjunctive tense and imperative. In all compound verbs,
including those whose verbal element is...داشتن دار *dāštan*
dār- 'to have', the subjunctive tense (5/16 above) is formed
with

present stem + personal endings

(i.e. there is no prefix ...بـیـ\...بـ *be-/bi-*). For the negative we
prefix ...نـ *ná-* (...نیـ *náy-* before a vowel) to the verbal
element of the affirmative. The imperative is derived from
the subjunctive in the normal manner (5/18):

...گوش کردن کنـ *guš kardan kon-* to listen:

... گوش کنم\کنی\کند *guš konam/koni/konad...*
I may listen (etc.)

...گوش نکنم\نکنی\نکند *guš nakonam/nakoni/nakonad...*
I may not listen (etc.)

گوش (نـ)کن\(نـ)کنید *guš (na)kon/(na)konid*
(don't) listen

باید گوش کنید *bāyad guš konid*
you must listen

These are the grammatically correct subjunctive forms for
compound verbs. However, with many compound verbs the
'ordinary' subjunctive (i.e. with the ...بـیـ\...بـ prefix) is also
used in the subjunctive and/or in the imperative:

...معاف کردن کنـ *mu'āf kardan kon-* to excuse:

باید او را معاف کنید\بکنید. *bāyad u rā mu'āf*
(bo)konid. You have to excuse him.

...گوش دادن دهـ *guš dādan deh-* to listen:

خوب گوش بدهید. *xub guš bedehid.* Listen well.

One important exception is the rhetorical question, which
usually has no subjunctive prefix in compound verbs:

...کار کردن کنـ *kār kardan kon-* to do

من چه کار کنم؟ *mán ce kār konam?* What can I do?

Polite forms. See 12/4 for the use of فرمودن فرما... *farmudan farmā-* as the verbal element of many compound verbs in polite speech.

Colloquial tenses. See 5/15. For the colloquial continuous present and past tenses of compound verbs, the non-verbal element stays with the second component verb of the tense:

دارم اینجا کار می‌کنم. ‹*dāram injā kār mi konam.*›
I'm working here.

داشتم آنجا کار می‌کردم. ‹*dāštam onjā kār mi kardam.*›
I was working there.

30. Passive voice

A verb in the passive voice indicates not what its subject (see 5/4 above) *does* but what its subject *undergoes*. A simple English example of a passive expression is 'The letter is being written.'

In Persian the passive can be formed only if the original verb is capable of taking a direct object (see 5/6 above), which then becomes the subject of the passive expression. The passive is made with the formula

past participle + شدن شو... *šodan šav-* 'to become'

(see 5/20 for the past participle). The verb شدن agrees with the subject in the normal way, and goes into the appropriate tense.

Simple verbs. For a simple verb (i.e. one with a one-word infinitive) the formula given above suffices. Tenses are formed as usual, allowing for an important difference in the subjunctive. Examples of tenses:

Past (5/8):

نامه نوشته شد. *nāme nevešte šod.*
The letter was written.

Present (5/10):

نامه نوشته می‌شود. *nāme nevešte mi šavad.*
The letter is being written.

128

Perfect (5/21):

نامه نوشته شده است. *nāme neveŝte ŝode ast.*
The letter has been written.

Future (5/27):

نامه نوشته خواهد شد. *nāme neveŝte xāhad ŝod.*
The letter will be written.

Subjunctive (5/16), the ...بـ *be-* prefix is usually omitted:

نامه باید نوشته شود. *nāme bāyad neveŝte ŝavad.*
The letter must be written.

Compound verbs. See 5/29 above. For compound verbs made with ...کنـ کردن *kardan kon-*, we replace this verb as a rule with the auxiliary شدن. In the examples given below, verbs are shown with the principal parts of their verbal element (5/10 above):

active (i.e. non-passive) گم کردن کنـ... *gom kardan kon-* to lose,
passive گم شدن شو... *gom ŝodan ŝav-* to be/get lost:

نامه گم شد. *nāme gom ŝod.* The letter was lost.

نامه گم شده است. *nāme gom ŝode ast.*
The letter has been lost.

شاید نامه گم شده باشد. *ŝāyad nāme gom ŝode bāŝad.*
Perhaps the letter has been lost.

گم شو! *gom ŝou!* Get lost!

active چاپ کردن کنـ... *cāp kardan kon-* to print,
passive چاپ شدن شو... *cāp ŝodan ŝav-* to be printed:

اگهی دیروز چاپ شد. *āgahi diruz cāp ŝod.*
The notice was printed yesterday.

In one or two verbs, کردن is replaced by another verb for the passive:

active گول کردن کنـ... *gul kardan kon-* to deceive,
passive گول خوردن خورـ... *gul xordan xor-* to be deceived

A similar thing occurs with other verbal elements of compound verbs, with certain verbs only:

active   ‫انجام دادن ده...‬   *anjām dādan deh-* to achieve,

passive   ‫انجام یافتن یاب...‬   *anjām yāftan yāb-* to be achieved

active   ‫به هم زدن زن...‬   *be ham zadan zan-* to disturb,

passive   ‫به هم خوردن خور...‬   *be ham xordan xor-* to be disturbed

But for most compound verbs made with verbs other than ‫کردن‬, the verb of the compound is put into the past participle and the auxiliary ‫شدن‬ is added:

active   ‫آتش زدن زن...‬   *āteš zadan zan-* to set on fire,

passive   ‫آتش زده شدن شو...‬   *āteš zade šodan šav-* to be set on fire:

‫ساختمان اشتباهاً آتش زده شد.‬   *sāxtemān eštebāhan āteš zade šod.* The building was accidentally set on fire.

active   ‫تصمیم گرفتن گیر...‬   *tasmim gereftan gir-* to decide,

passive ‫تصمیم گرفته شدن شو...‬   *tasmim gerefte šodan šav-* to be decided

‫تصمیم گرفته شد که ...‬   *tasmim gerefte šod ke ...* It was decided that …

The negative of the passive of all verbs, both simple and compound, is made by negating the auxiliary ‫شدن‬ in the normal manner, i.e.:

- prefixing ‫نـ...‬ *ná-* (stressed) to the auxiliary in the past tense, imperative, perfect, perfect subjunctive, pluperfect and future tenses:

‫نامه امروز نوشته نشد.‬   *nāme emruz nevešte nášod.* The letter was not written today.

‫گم نشو!‬   *gom nášou!* Don't get lost!

‫پول هنوز پیدا نشده است.‬   *pul hanuz peidā nášode ast.* The money has not yet been found.

‫تصمیم گرفته نشده بود.‬   *tasmim gerefte nášode bud.* It had not been decided.

‫نامه امروز امضا نخواهد شد.‬   *nāme emruz emzā náxāhad šod.* The letter will not be signed today.

- prefixing ‫نـ...‬ *né-/ná-* (stressed) to the auxiliary in the present and the imperfect tenses:

نامه امروز فرستاده نمی‌شود. *nāme emruz ferestāde némi šavad.* The letter is not being/will not be sent today.

Several things are worth noting about the Persian passive in general:

- All the parts of the passive verb stay together, usually at the end of the sentence or clause (see 8/4 for the definition of a clause).

- Although we can add to the passive verb the instrument with which an action was done:

پنجره با آجر شکسته شد. *panjare bā ājor šekaste šod.* The window was broken with a brick.

we cannot add the person by whom it was done. The correct rendering of 'The window was broken by a thief' in Persian is with an active sentence:

دزدی پنجره را شکست. *dozdi panjare rā šekast.* A thief broke the window.

- We cannot make a passive of the English type 'I was given a present'; only the direct object may become the subject of the passive verb. This sentence is best expressed in Persian impersonally:

هدیه به من دادند. *hadiye be man dādand.* They gave me a present.

or, more heavily, a passive with the old direct object 'a present' as subject of the passive verb:

هدیه به من داده شد. *hadiye be man dāde šod.* A present was given to me.

- The versatile nature of some past participles can cause confusion. Contrast these sentences containing the past participle بسته *baste* 'closed':

  - Active verb, perfect tense:

تاجر دکان را بسته است. *tājer dokkān rā baste ast.* The merchant has closed the shop.

131

- Past participle used as an adjective, indicating a state, not an action:

دکان بسته است. *dokkān baste ast.* The shop is closed.

- Passive verb, perfect tense:

دکان بسته شده است. *dokkān baste šode ast.*

  The shop has been (and still is) closed.

6. Prepositions

1. General

A preposition shows the relationship between the noun (3/1) or pronoun (4/1) following it and the rest of the sentence. The preposition is said to *govern* its noun or pronoun:

در ایران زندگی می‌کنیم. *dar irān zendegi mi konim.*
We live in Iran.

بشقاب روی میز است. *bošqāb ruye miz ast.*
The plate is on the table.

جز من کسی نیست. *joz man kasi nist.*
There's nobody except me.

See 4/4 for the use of prepositions with personal pronouns.

2. Basic prepositions

Persian has few basic prepositions. They are all short words, and are all followed directly by the expression which they govern:

در	*dar* in(to)	از	*az* from, by, through, since, than
به	*be* to	بر	*bar* on (figuratively)
با	*bā* with, despite	بی	*bi* without
تا	*tā* as far as, until	جز	*joz* except
		چون	*cun* like

در کلاس سوم *dar kelāse sevvom* in Class Three
('in the third class')

با آنها رفتم. *bā ānhā raftam.* I went with them.

تا گوشه رفتند و ایستادند. *tā guše raftand va istādand.*
They went as far as the corner and stopped/stood.

دیروز به شهر رسید. *diruz be šahr rasid.*
He/She arrived in ('to') town yesterday.

از من نام و نشانیم را پرسیدند. *az man nām va nešāniam rā*
porsidand. They asked ('from') me my name and address.

Note:
- We also encounter ...بـ *be-* (with no ه) joined to the next

133

word, in older printed and handwritten Persian:

به فرودگاه (earlier, بفرودگاه) *be forudgāh* to the airport

به آنها (earlier, باآنها) *be ānhā* to them

The combinations به این *be in* 'to this, to these' and به آن *be ān* 'to that, to those' have also the less frequent alternative forms بدین *bedin* and بدان *bedān*.

See 6/6 below for more about *be* in everyday speech.

- The preposition *bi* 'without' is often written as a joined prefix in compound words (11/2, 3):

بیکار *bikār* ('without work') unemployed

بیکاری *bikāri* unemployment

بیچاره *bicāre* ('without remedy') helpless

بیچارگی *bicāregi* helplessness

- Some important compound prepositions are formed with these basic ones:

پیش از\قبل از *piš az/qabl az* before

بعد از\پس از *ba'd az/pas az* after

راجع به *raje' be* concerning

بنا بر *banā bar* in accordance with

- Some of the commoner basic prepositions are used together with an abstract noun to form adverbs (7/2):

به ندرت *be nodrat* rarely

در نتیجه *dar natije* consequently

- See 5/6 for prepositional objects after verbs.

See 6/3 below for more about در *dar*.

See 3/9 for از *az* and تا *tā* meaning 'than'.

3 . Prepositions with اضافه *ezāfe*

Many prepositions are followed by the *ezāfe* (see Appendix II). These are mostly other parts of speech, or compounds made with other parts of speech, used as prepositions.

All these are best learned together with the *ezāfe* which follows them. Essential ones include:

برای	barāye ‹bare› for		توی*	tuye in(to)
روی	ruye on		بدون	bedune without
جلوی	jelouye in front of		عقب	aqabe behind
پیش	piše in front of		پشت	pošte behind
داخل	dāxele inside		خارج	xāreje outside
طرف	tarafe towards (a place)		پیش	piše towards (a person)
به جای	be jāye instead of		با وجود	bā vojude in spite of
بالای	bālāye above		زیر	zire below
در بارهٔ	dar bāreye concerning		به سبب	be sababe because of
سر	sare on top of		در کنار	dar kenāre along
بین	beine between		در میان	dar miāne among

برای بچه ها درستش کردم. barāye baccehā dorošteš kardam.
I made it for the children.

داخل خانه صدایی نیست. dāxele xāne sedāi nist.
Inside the house there is no sound.

گاهی پیش پدرم می آمد. gāhi piše pedaram mi āmad.
Sometimes he came to my father.

اتوبوس جلوی سفارت می ایستد. otobus jelouye sefārat
mi istad. The bus stops in front of the embassy.

توی* tuye is often used in everyday speech instead of در dar (3/2
above) for 'in(to)', with literal or physical meaning. For figurative
meaning, and with names of towns and countries, در dar is used in
speech as in writing:

توی خانه اش tuye xāneaš in his/her house

دزد توی کوچه فرار کرد. dozd tuye kuce farār kard.
The thief fled up ('into') the alley.

but: در این حال dar in hāl in this case/this instance

در شیراز\در ایران dar širāz/dar irān in Shiraz/in Iran

4. Prepositions and conjunctions

A preposition governs a noun or pronoun; a conjunction introduces
a clause, which is a group of words making at least limited sense

and centred on a verb with its subject (see 8/4). It is important not to confuse the two types of word or expression, especially as in some cases (in Persian or in English) they may be similar. Typical pairs, with references for the conjunctions, are:

Preposition + noun/pronoun	Conjunction + clause
قبـل از *qabl az* before قبل از مذاکره *qabl az mozākere* before the conference	قبـل از اینکه *qabl az inke* before قبل از اینکه بروید *qabl az inke beravid* before you go/went 8/9
بعد از *ba'd az* after بعد از درس *ba'd az dars* after the lesson	بعد از اینکه *ba'd az inke* after بعد از اینکه رسیدند *ba'd az inke rasidand* after they arrive(d) 8/9
بـه سبب *be sababe* because of به سبب آن *be sababe ān* because of that	بـرای اینکه *barāye inke* because برای اینکه فراموش کرد *barāye inke farāmuš kard* because he forgot 8/10
در صورت *dar surate* in case of در صورت اشکال *dar surate eškāl* in case of difficulty	در صورتی که *dar surati ke* if, in case در صورتی که اشکال باشد *dar surati ke eškāl bāšad* if/in case there is difficulty 8/11

The most important types of clause, including those introduced by the conjunctions shown above, are explained in 8/5 to 13.

5. Prepositions governing other expressions

A preposition can also govern an expression of time or place, where the meaning permits:

این را به بالا ببر. *in rā be bālā bebar.* Take this upstairs.

تا حالا شکایتی نبوده است. *tā hālā šekāyati nabude ast.*
Until now there has been no complaint.

از اینجا دور است. *az injā dur ast ‹e›.* It is far from here.

6 . Omission of به *be*

In colloquial language it is common, in simple sentences with a verb of motion, to omit the preposition به *be* 'to' and to put the verb before the destination:

می روم منزل. ‹*mi ram manzel*›. I'm going home.

کی می آیند شیراز؟ ‹*kei mi ānd širāz*›?
When are they coming to Shiraz?

شیراز، آرامگاه حافظ *širāz - ārāmgāhe hāfez*
Shiraz - Hafez' Tomb

137

7. Adverbs

1. General

Adverbs are words which are said to 'modify' a verb (5/1), an adjective (3/6), or another adverb. They state or ask in what manner or circumstances the verb, adjective or other adverb applies:

اینجا زندگی می‌کنند. _injā_ zendegi mi konand.
They live <u>here</u>.

آیا تهران خیلی بزرگ است؟ _āyā tehrān <u>xeili</u> bozorg ast?_
Is Tehran <u>very</u> big?

او کمی بهتر می خواند. _u <u>kami</u> behtar mi xānad._
He reads <u>a little</u> better.

2. Forming adverbs

Most adverbs of _manner_ (i.e. those showing how a verb applies) and many adverbs of _time_ (showing when a verb applies) are identical to the adjectives with related meaning. Compare adjective and adverb:

کارش خوب است. _kāreš xub ast._ His/Her work is good.

خوب کار می‌کند. _xub kār mi konad._ He/She works well.

Similarly: زود می‌رسند. _zud mi rasand._ They are arriving soon.

آهسته حرف می‌زند. _āheste harf mi zanad._
He/She talks slowly.

معلم تند می نویسد. _mo'allem tond mi nevisad._
The teacher writes fast.

بد گذشت. _bad gozašt._ It went off badly.

او کتاب زیاد دوست دارد. _u ketāb ziād dust dārad._
She likes books a lot.

تنها زندگی می‌کند. _tanhā zendegi mi konad._
He/She lives alone.

مذاکره ششماهه منعقد می‌شود. _mozākere šešmāhe mon'aqed mi šavad_ The conference is held six-monthly.

Some adverbs have the form of a phrase:

با دقت *bā deqqat* accurately ('with accuracy')

با هم *bā ham* together

دست کم *daste kam* at least

به زودی *be zudí* quickly

به ویژه *be viže* especially

A few adjectives have to add ...انه *-āne* to become adverbs of manner:

خوشبخت *xošbaxt* lucky   خوشبختانه *xošbaxtāne* fortunately

بدبخت *badbaxt* unlucky   بدبختانه *badbaxtāne* unfortunately

متأسف\متاسف *mota(')assef* sorry

متأسفانه\متاسفانه *mota(')assefāne* regretfully

Other types of adverbs (adverbs of place, adverbs of degree, and some adverbs of time; there is no need to distinguish, as they can all be studied together) do not for the most part have related adjectives. Important adverbs of these types include:

اینجا *injā* here   آنجا *ānjā* there

اینطور\چنین *intour/conin* thus, like this, so   آنطور\چنان *āntour/conān* thus, like that, so

حالا\اکنون *hālā/aknun* now   آنوقت *ānvaqt* then

خیلی\بسیار *xeili/besyār* very   کم\کمی *kam(i)* (a) little

هم *ham* also   همیشه *hamiše* always

هیچوقت\هرگز *hicvaqt/hargez* never (with negative verb)

گاهی\بعضی اوقات\بعضی وقتها *gāhi/ba'zi ouqāt/ba'zi vaqthā* sometimes

بارها *bārhā* often   هرگاه *hargāh* everywhere

هیچ جا *hic jā* nowhere (with negative verb)

بیرون *birun* outside   داخل *dāxel* inside

جلو\پیش *jelou/piš* forward(s)   عقب *aqab* back(wards)

بالا *bālā* up   پایین *pāin* down

(یک) قدری *(yek) qadri* a little

140

بالا نگاه نکن. *bālā negāh nakon.* Don't look up.

چنان خراب شد که ... *conān xarāb šod ke ...*
It was so (badly) damaged that ...

این اشخاص همیشه دروغ می گویند. *in ašxās hamiše doruq*
mi guyand. These people always lie.

بیرون کسی هست. *birun kasi hast.*
There's someone outside.

گاهی اتفاق می‌افتاد که... *gāhi ettefāq mi oftād ke ...*
Sometimes it happened that ...

هیچ جا پیدا نشد. *hic jā peidā našod.*
('It was found nowhere.') It was nowhere to be found.

این جور پیشنهاد را هیچوقت قبول نمی کنید.
in jur pišnehād rā hicvaqt qabul nemi konid.
You will never accept a proposal of this kind.

Adverbs beginning with ...این *in-* and ...آن *ān* can be strengthened
by prefixing ...همـ *hám-*; this syllable then takes the stress of the
word:

همینجا زندگی می کردند. *háminjā zendegi mi kardand.*
They used to live (just) here.

همینطور خوب است. ‹*hámintour xub e.*› Just like that is fine.

Many adverbs taken from Arabic end in the form اً... *án* (stressed;
see also 1/23); those derived from a word ending in ...ی drop this
ending before اً...:

مخصوصاً *maxsusan* especially		خصوصاً *xosusan* privately
عموماً *omuman* publicly		تقریباً *taqriban* approximately
تماماً *tamāman* completely		سابقاً *sābeqan* formerly
معمولاً *ma'mulan* usually		حتماً *hatman* certainly
قبلاً *qablan* previously		بعداً *ba'dan* afterwards
شخصاً *šaxsan* personally		اصلاً *aslan* essentially
		غالباً *qāleban* mostly

The adverbial numbers shown in 9/6 (اولاً *avvalan* 'firstly' etc.) also
belong to this group.

Those adverbs derived from words ending in ت... *-at* or in *-e* +

silent ه (1/15) replace this ending with تـ... -atán:

حقيقتًا *haqiqatan* in truth نسبتًا *nesbatan* relatively

قاعدتًا *qā'edatan* as a rule

The forms in تـ... -atan are now less common; for most of them a phrase is preferred:

به نسبت *be nesbat* relatively در حقيقت *dar haqiqat* in truth

Also, in older texts and in some dictionaries we still find the original Arabic spelling of -atan, ة... (نسبةً, حقيقةً).

Some important phrases are taken from Arabic, many of them serving as adverbs of manner. They tend to keep their Arabic spelling. Important ones are:

فوق العاده *fouqal'āde* exceptionally الآن *alān ‹alón›* now

بالأخره\بالاخره *belaxere* finally فى الفور *felfour* immediately

It is simplest to learn these as vocabulary, transcribing each as a single word.

Some noun expressions of time operate as adverbs. There is usually no preposition, and often the noun is plural:

روز جمعه آمدوشد كم است. *ruze jom'e āmadošod kam ast.*
(On) Friday the traffic is slight.

صبحها زود بيدار مى شويم. *sobhhā zud bidār mi šavim.*
(In the) morning we wake early.

بعد از ظهرها مردم پير استراحت مى كنند. *ba'd az zohrhā mardome pir esterāhat mi konand.*
(In the) afternoon(s) the old people rest.

ساعت چند مى رسند؟ *sā'ate cand mi rasand?*
(At) what time are they arriving?

Adverbs modifying an adjective in a construction with *ezāfe* interrupt the construction (see 3/8):

اين مسئلهٔ خيلى\بسيار مهم *in mas'aleye xeili/besyār mohem*
this very important problem

كتاب كمى مشكلى ست. *ketābe kami moškeli st.*
It is a rather difficult book.

142

3. Comparative and superlative of adverbs

See 3/9, 10. An adverb whose meaning permits it can be made comparative and superlative. The comparative form is the same as for adjectives:

او بهتر از دیگران کار می‌کند. *u behtar az digarān kār mi konad.* He/She works better than the others.

در این مغازه ارزانتر می فروشند. *dar in maqāze arzāntar mi forušand.* They sell more cheaply in this shop.

Equal comparison is expressed with به *be* and an abstract noun, following the formula shown in 3/9:

پروین به سرعت بچه‌های بزرگتر (ن)می‌دود. *parvin be sor'ate baccehāye bozorgtar (ne)mi davad.* Parvin runs/doesn't run as fast as (the) older ('bigger') children.

For the superlative, we use از همه *az hame* with the comparative:

آنها از همه زودتر رسیدند. *ānhā az hame zudtar rasidand.* They arrived the earliest ('sooner than all').

as ... as possible. The idiom 'as ... as possible' is expressed in Persian with هر چه + the comparative, ...تر هر چه *har ce -tar*:

هر چه زودتر بیا. *har ce zudtar biā.* Come as quickly as possible.

4. Interrogative adverbs

Important interrogative adverbs are:

چطور *cetour* how   چرا *cerā* why

کجا *kojā* where   کی *kei* when

چند وقت *cand vaqt* for how long   چقدر *ceqadr* how greatly

این را چطور درست می‌کنند؟ *in rā cetour dorost mi konand?* How do they make this?

همکارتان کی بر می‌گردد؟ *hamkāretān kei bar mi gardad?* When is your colleague returning?

کجا درس خواندید؟ *kojā dars xāndid?* Where did you study?

See 8/2 for the order of words in the question.

5. Order of adverbs

When adverbs of different types occur in a sentence, the three main types appear in the order *time-manner-place*. A simple mnemonic for this is the word *tempo*.

امروز تنها بیرون رفتم. *emruz tanhā birun raftam.*
Today I went out alone.

6. Adverbial participles

The commonest participles are verbal *adjectives* (5/20), used as adjectives or nouns, or to form the perfect tenses. Persian has also adverbial participles (also called participles of manner), derived from the verb on the formula present stem + *-ān* (see 5/10 for the present stem). The adverbial participle expresses an action or state accompanying the verb.

خندیدن خند.... *xandidan xand-* to laugh:

خندان گفت... *xandān goft...* She said, with a laugh ('laughing')...

This form of participle is not common.

تخت جمشید *taxte jamšid* Persepolis

8. Syntax

1. General

Chapters 3 to 7 and Chapters 9 and 12 cover those points of syntax (i.e. sentence structure) which can conveniently be covered there; this chapter covers only those points which cannot.

2. Questions

Questions expecting the answer 'yes' or 'no'. A statement is made into a question of this sort by adding the particle آيا *áyā* at the beginning, and raising the voice briefly on the stressed syllable of the word which is questioned, then dropping it again slightly. The order of words in the rest of the sentence does not change:

حاضريد. *hāzérid.* You're ready. (statement)

آيا حاضريد ؟ *āyā hāzérid?* Are you ready?

كسى نيامد. *kasi náyāmad* ‹*náyumad*›. Nobody came.

آيا كسى نيامد؟ *āyā kasi náyāmad?* Did nobody come?

آيا اينجا مى آيند ؟ *āyā injā mi āyand?* Are they coming here?

آيا انگليسى صحبت مى فرماييد*؟ *āyā englisi sohbat mi farmāid?* Do you speak English?

* Polite speech, see 12/4.

In speech it is common to omit the particle آيا *āyā:*

حاضريد؟ *hāzerid?*

كسى نيامد؟ *kasi nayāmad?*

and/or to add يا نه *yā ná* 'or not' (note the stress) at the end. The intonation is the same; further, the expression does not in any way imply impatience or annoyance as does its English counterpart:

حاضريد يا نه؟ *hāzerid yā na?* Are you ready?

In reply to an affirmative question, 'yes' is بله *bále:*

(آيا)حاضريد؟ - بله (حاضرم). *(āyā) hāzerid? - bale (hāzeram).* Are you ready? - Yes (I am).

145

In reply to a negative question, 'yes' is چرا *cérā*:

؟(حاضرم) چرا – حاضر نیستید *hāzer nistid? - cerā (hāzeram).*
Aren't you ready? - Yes (I am).

'No' is نه *na*, or more emphatically نخیر *náxeir*:

؟(است) پست رسیده *post raside (ast)?* Has the mail arrived?

.نخیر ، هنوز نرسیده – *- naxeir, hanuz naraside.* - No, not yet.

Questions expecting a *contrary* yes-no answer are often introduced by مگر *mágar*, which implies 'really ...?'. The particle آیا *āyā* is then dropped. The intonation is the same as for a normal yes-no question:

؟مگر شما نرفتید *magar šomā naraftid?* Did you (really) not go?
(negative question, expecting the answer 'yes')

؟مگر شما رفتید *magar šomā raftid?* Did you (really) go?
(affirmative question, expecting the answer 'no')

Note the first-syllable stress on *áyā*, *bále*, *cérā*, *náxeir* and *mágar*.

Questions not expecting the answer 'yes' or 'no'. Questions other than yes-no questions focus on the appropriate interrogative word or expression. The word or expression may be an interrogative adjective with its noun (3/13), an interrogative pronoun (4/7) or an interrogative adverb (7/4). For convenience the main ones are listed here also:

adjectives: کدام *kodām ‹kodum›* which   چه *ce* what (kind of)

چطور\چگونه\چه جور\چه نوع *cetour/cegune/ce jur/ce nou'*
what kind of

چند *cand* how much/many

pronouns: کی *ki* who   چه *ce ‹ci›* what

مال کی *māle ki* whose   چقدر *ceqadr* how much

adverbs: کی *kei* when   کجا *kojā* where

چطور *cetour* how   چرا *cerā* why

چند وقت *cand vaqt* (for) how long.

In such questions the interrogative word or expression stands immediately before the verb or before any adverb(s) accompanying the verb. چرا *cerā* 'why' and کی *ki* 'who' are exceptions; they usually begin the question. The voice rises momentarily on the stressed syllable of the interrogative word:

او چطور مدیریست؟ *u cetour modirist?*
What sort of a manager is he?

این به شما چطور کمک می‌کند؟ *in be šomā cetour komak ‹mi kone›?* How does that ('this') help you?

برای تعطیلات کجا می‌روند؟ *barāye ta'tilāt kojā mi ravand ‹mi rand›?* Where are they going for their holiday?

کی به شما اینطور گفت؟ *ki be šomā intour goft?*
Who told you so?

چرا حساب را قبول نکرد؟ *cerā hesāb rā qabul nakard?*
Why didn't he accept the account(s)?

با کی کار دارید؟ *bā ki kār dārid?*
('With whom do you have business?') Whom do you want?

3. Indirect speech

Direct speech is the words of the original speaker quoted verbatim. It is usually shown in quotation marks in English: He said 'I am ill.' It presents no problem in Persian, though the quotation marks are often missing:

گفت مریضم. *goft marizam.* He/She said 'I am ill.'

Indirect speech (also called reported speech) does not quote verbatim; it paraphrases. The indirect-speech form of the English sentence shown above would be: He said that he was ill.

Indirect speech can be divided into indirect statement, indirect question and indirect command.

Indirect statement. Examples of Persian indirect statement:

می‌گوید که مریض است. *mi guyad ke mariz ast.*
He/She says (that) he/she is ill.

گفت که مریض است. *goft ke mariz ast.*
He/She said that he/she was ill.

گزارش دادند که معلم غایب بود.

gozāreš dādand ke mo'allem qāyeb bud.

They reported that the teacher had been ('was') absent.

دوباره گفتند که خواهند آمد. *dobāre goftand ke xāhand āmad.*

They repeated that they would ('will') come.

محمد نوشت که درو عالی بوده (است).

mohammad nevešt ke derou āli bude (ast).

Mohammad wrote that the harvest had been ('has been') excellent.

Things to note:

- The conjunction که *ke* 'that' cannot properly be left out, as can 'that' in English. In everyday speech some Iranians drop it; but not consistently, and it is risky to imitate this until one is sure of the context.

- The tense of the verb is that of the original direct speech.

The indirect statement construction applies not only to statements depending on verbs of speech proper, but also to facts or alleged facts depending on verbs of perception or feeling, as in English:

فکر می کردیم که نمی آیید. *fekr mi kardim ke nemi āid.*

We thought you weren't coming.

می دانستند که دروغ می گوید. *mi dānestand ‹mi dunestand› ke doruq mi guyad ‹mi ge›.* They knew he was lying.

یقین دارم که گم می شود. *yaqin dāram ke gom mi šavad ‹mi še›.* I am certain it will be lost.

شنیدم که پسرتان بر گشتند*. *šenidam ke pesaretān bar gaštand.* I heard that your son had returned.

* Polite speech, see 12/3.

Indirect question. Direct questions are examined in 8/2 above. Indirect questions follow the same general rules as indirect statements. Indirect questions of the 'yes-no' type are introduced by آیا *áyā* or که آیا *ke áyā*, both meaning 'whether'. Often both introductory words are left out, and/or the expression یا نه *yā ná* 'or not' (see 8/2 above) is added:

پرسیدم (که) آیا او مریض است. porsidam (ke) āyā u mariz
ast ‹e›.

پرسیدم مریض است یا نه. porsidam mariz ast yā na.
I asked whether he/she was ill.

Other questions are introduced by the appropriate interrogative
word or by که plus the interrogative word:

پرسیدم (که) کی می آیند. porsidam (ke) kei mi āyand
‹mi ānd›. I asked when they were coming.

پرسیدم چرا استعفا می‌دهد. porsidam cerā este'fā mi dehad.
I asked why he was resigning.

Indirect questions occur also after verbs of statement, perception
or feeling:

شرح دادم چرا استعفا می‌دهم. šarh dādam cerā este'fā
mi deham. I explained why I was resigning.

می‌دانید چرا استعفا داده است؟ mi dānid cerā este'fā dāde ast?
Do you know why he has resigned?

نمی‌فهمم چطور شد. nemi fahmam cetour šod.
I don't understand how it happened ('became').

Indirect command. Direct command or request is the imperative,
explained in 5/18. Indirect command or request is expressed with
(که +) subjunctive (5/16) observing the formula 'I asked that he
should ...':

افسر به سربازان فرمود که حمله کنند.
afsar be sarbāzān farmud ke hamle konand.
The officer ordered the troops to attack ('that they attack').

خواهش کردم (که) زود تشریف بیاورند*.
xāheš kardam (ke) zud tašrif biāvarand ‹biāran›.
I asked him/her to come ('that he/she should come') soon.

* Polite speech, see 12/4.

4. Clauses - general

In 8/5 to 13 below, and elsewhere, there is reference to *clauses*. A
clause is a group of words making at least partial sense, centred

on a verb (5/1) with its subject (4/2, 5/4). We distinguish between a *main* clause, which usually makes complete sense, and a *dependent* clause, which usually adds meaning to the main clause (or to another dependent clause) and makes only limited sense by itself. In the English sentence 'This is the house that Jack built' the first four words are the main clause, the last three a dependent clause describing 'house'. A dependent clause is almost always introduced by a *conjunction* (or another part of speech acting as a conjunction); in some circumstances this may be omitted. We examine below noun clauses, relative clauses and clauses of purpose, result, time, reason, condition, concession and manner.

ماهان، دختران جوان   *māhān - doxtarāne javān*
Mahan - Young girls

5. Noun clauses

See 8/4 above. Examine the sentences:

ممکن است (که) بیاید.   *momken ast (ke) biāyad ‹biād›.*
It is possible (that) he may come.

یقین نیست که بلد باشند.   *yaqin nist ke balad bāšand.*
It is not certain that they are aware (of it).

150

The clause introduced by که *ke* in these examples is a noun clause, so called because it is an extended subject of the verb است *ast* or نیست *nist*: 'that he may come' is possible; 'that they are aware of it' is uncertain. The verb in the noun clause itself is in the subjunctive (see 5/16) because it is an idea, not a fact. The formula is therefore که + subjunctive.

After some common expressions such as ممکن است *momken ast* 'It is possible', the conjunction که *ke* may be omitted. It is safest for our purposes to keep it.

In sentences with noun clauses, the main clause may express the attitude of the speaker to the prospect or situation:

حیف است که برف نباشد. *heif ast ke barf nabāšad.*
It's a pity (that) there is ('should be') no snow.

Here the absence of the snow is a fact; but the verb نباشد *nabāšad* stands in the subjunctive because it is the idea itself, fact or not, which is regretted.

The noun clause may in other examples be the *object* of the main verb:

خوشوقتیم (که) بیاید ‹بیآد›. *xošvaqtim (ke) biāyad ‹biād›.*
We are pleased (that) he is coming.

امیدوارم (که) زود برسند. *omidvāram (ke) zud berasand.*
I hope they arrive soon.

ناراحتم که بچه‌ها تنها بمانند. *nārāhatam ke baccehā tanhā bemānand.* I am uneasy that the children should remain alone.

آیا می‌ترسیدند که بیماری منتشر شود؟ *āyā mi tarsidand ke bimāri montašer šavad?* Did they fear the sickness would spread?

Sentiments such as 'I am anxious that … not' are also expressed with ترسیدن ترس... *tarsidan tars-* 'to fear' and مبادا *mabādā* + subjunctive. The verb is affirmative; the negative is contained in the conjunction مبادا *mabādā* 'lest':

می‌ترسم مبادا مریض بشوید. *mi tarsam mabādā mariz bešavid.*
I am anxious that you should not fall ill ('lest you fall ill').

151

(For the record, the clauses of indirect speech, see 8/3 above, are also grammatically speaking noun-object clauses; but it is simpler to restrict the term 'noun clauses' to the type shown here.)

6 . Relative clauses

See 8/4 above. In a sentence such as 'The man who wrote this became famous' the clause 'who wrote this' is a *relative* clause, relating to, identifying or describing an *antecedent* which is in this case the noun 'man'. The relative clause is introduced by a *relative pronoun* (also known as a relative conjunction).

The common English relative pronouns are 'who', 'whom', 'which', 'that', 'whose'. In some sentences they can be omitted: 'The book (which) I bought ...' The Persian relative pronoun is که *ke* (sometimes چه *ce*), and in principle it is not omitted.

Noun antecedents. In the commonest kind of relative sentence the antecedent is a noun, and carries the suffix ...ی . This is the <u>relative -i</u>*, which is distinct from the indefinite -i* explained in 3/2, but it is written in the same manner. It has no effect on the stress of the word.

مردی که این را نوشت معروف شد. *mardi ke in rā nevešt ma'ruf šod.* The man who wrote this became famous.

حزبی که آن برنامه را قبول می‌کند حتماً انتخاب می‌شود. *hezbi ke ān barnāme rā qabul mi konad hatman entexāb mi šavad.* The party which adopts that programme will certainly be elected.

In these examples, both the antecedent and the relative که are the *subject* of their respective verbs. When either one is the *direct object* (5/6) of its verb, we can add, optionally, the direct-object suffix را *rā** after the relative ...ی *-i*:

کوزه‌ای (را) که از بازار آوردم کجاست؟ *kuzei (rā) ke az bāzār āvordam kojāst?* Where is the pot that I brought from the market?

کتابهایی (را) که خریدم گم کردم. *ketābhāi (rā) ke xaridam gom kardam.* I have lost the books that I bought.

152

برنامهٔ جدیدی (را) که حزب قبول کرد بیفایده به نظر می‌آید.

barnāmeye jadidi (rā) ke hezb qabul kard bifāyede be nazar mi āyad. The new programme which the party has adopted seems useless.

کتابی (را) که خریدم مفید است. *ketābi (rā) ke xaridam*

mofid ‹e›. The book (which) I bought is useful.

In sentences with the pattern 'This is the person who ...', the first verb is put at the end of its own clause, separating the antecedent from the relative که:

این شخصی است که دیروز آمد. *in šaxsi st ke diruz āmad.*

This is the person who came yesterday.

(not: [. این شخصی که دیروز آمد است.])

این کتابی است که من خریدم. *in ketābi st ke man xaridam.*

This is the book (which) I bought.

* The uses of the suffixes ی... *-i* and را *rā* are summarised in Appendices III and IV respectively.

Prepositional or possessive relative. See 6/2, 3 and 3/11. A relative clause with prepositional or possessive relationship ('to whom', 'from which', 'whose' etc. in English) is still introduced in Persian with که, but we put the appropriate preposition or possessive adjective in the relative clause. The preposition gets its own 'repeat' pronoun:

پسری که به او نامه‌را دادم بر گشته است.

pesari ke be u ‹ke beš› nāme rā dādam bar gašte ast. The boy to whom I gave the letter ('who I gave the letter to him') has returned.

این خانه‌ایست که در آن زندگی می‌کرد.

in xāneist ke dar ān zendegi mi kard. This is the house in which ('which in it') he/she lived.

با بچه‌هایی که مادر آنها\مادرشان مریض شد صحبت کرده ایم.

bā baccehāi ke mādare ānhā/mādarešān mariz šod sohbat karde im. We have spoken to the children whose mother ('who their mother') has fallen ill.

دزدی(را)که دنبالش دویدند گرفته اند یا نه؟

dozdi (ra) ke dombāleš davidand gerefte and yā na? Have they caught the thief they ran after?

Pronoun antecedents. Relative expressions with pronoun antecedents mostly differ from those with noun antecedents, and are best learned by example.

آنهایی که *ānhāi ke* 'those who' is the only example of a pronoun antecedent following completely the noun-antecedent model:

آنهایی که اینطور فکر می‌کنند دیوانه هستند. *ānhāi ke intour fekr mi konand divāne hastand.* Those who think so are mad.

آنهایی را که نپرداختند قبول نمی‌کنیم. *ānhāi rā ke napardāxtand qabul nemi konim.* We shall not accept those who did not pay.

آنهایی که بلیط داشتند داخل شدند. *ānhāi ke belit dāštand dāxel šodand.* Those who had a ticket came in.

The following pronoun antecedents have the relative pronoun که *ke* for persons and چه *ce* for things; there is no relative -*i*. Note the alternative spellings. Apart from these points, the rules for noun antecedents apply. Each antecedent is shown with its relative pronoun:

آن که\آنکه *ān ke* he who   هر که *har ke* whoever

آن چه\آنچه *ān ce* that which, what   هر چه *har ce* whatever

آنکه\هر که اینطور می‌گوید اشتباه می‌کند. *ān ke/har ke intour mi guyad eštebāh mi konad.* He who/Whoever says that ('thus') is mistaken.

آنچه مرا ناراحت می‌کند بیکاری جوانان است. *ān ce marā nārāhat mi konad bikāriye javānan ast.* What ('That which') worries me is youth unemployment.

هر چه میل می‌فرمایید* ببرید. *har ce meil mi farmāid bebarid.* Take whatever you want.

* Polite speech, see 12/4.

Non-identifying relatives. The relative expressions examined above are all 'identifying' relatives. By contrast, a non-identifying relative clause does not single out the antecedent; it merely gives some information about it. There is no relative -*i*. Examine:

این آموزگار که برادرم است ... *in āmuzgār ke barādaram ast ...* This teacher, who is my brother, ...

154

اصفهان که آنوقت پایتخت کشور بود ...

esfahan ke ānvaqt pāitaxte kešvar bud ...

Isfahan, which at that time was the capital of the country, ...

از آقای هیوی که رئیس کمیته بودند پرسیدند.

az āqāye hayavi ke ra'ise komite budand porsidand.

They asked Mr Hayavi, who was the chairman of the committee.

In the last sentence, که *ke* 'who' implies 'because he' or 'who, as we know, ...'.

Relative with subjunctive. When it is not certain that the relative clause reflects a fact, it is common to put its verb in the subjunctive (5/16). There is no relative *-i*; the *-i* of the following examples is *indefinite*, not *relative*:

آیا کسی هست که فارسی بلد باشد؟ *āyā kasi hast ke fārsi balad bāšad?* Is there someone who knows Persian?

کسی نیست که به ایشان کمک کند. *kasi nist ke be išān komak konad.* There is nobody who will/nobody to help them.

من شاگردانی می‌خواهم که خوب کار کنند. *man šāgerdāni mi xāham ke xub kār konand.* I want pupils who (will) work well.

Contrast this last sentence expressing an uncertainty with a similar sentence expressing a fact, in which the verb stands in a non-subjunctive tense:

در این کلاس شاگردانی هستند که خوب کار می‌کنند. *dar in kelās šāgerdāni hastand ke xub kar mi konand.* In this class there are pupils who work well.

Emphatic *ke*. In colloquial language we can add a non-identifying *ke* after a noun or pronoun, for emphasis or simply to announce the subject. The sentence has an air of protest, and the *ke* has no relative meaning at all:

خسرو که دیگر رفته. ‹*xosrou ke dige rafte.*› Khosrow - he's gone.

ما که نمی‌دانیم دیگر. ‹*mā ke nemi dunim dige.*› Well, *we* don't know.

155

7. Clauses of purpose

See 8/4 above. Clauses showing with what purpose the action of the main verb is or was performed are introduced by one of the conjunctions

تا *tā* so that   برای اینکه *barāye inke* so that

مبادا *mabādā* lest, so that ... not   که *ke* (less common) so that

The verb in the purpose clause stands in the subjunctive (5/16):

زود بروید تا\برای اینکه سر وقت برسید. *zud beravid tā/barāye inke sare vaqt berasid.* Go quickly so that you arrive on time.

خوب بنویسید مبادا فراموش کنید. *xub benevisid mabādā farāmuš konid.* Write (it) properly ('well') so that you do not forget.

In English we can often express purpose with 'in order to' and an infinitive; in Persian we have to have a subject plus verb, i.e. a clause:

صبر کردیم تا\که وزیر را ببینیم. *sabr kardim tā/ke vazir rā bebinim.* We waited in order to ('so that we might') see the minister.

8. Clauses of result

See 8/4 above. Clauses showing the result of the action of the main verb are introduced by one of the conjunctions

چنان ... که *conān ... ke* so ... that

آنقدر ... که *ānqadr ... ke* so much ... that

in which the first element stands in the main clause and the که heads the result clause:

چنان تنبل بود که اخراج شد. *conān tambal bud ke exrāj šod.* He was so lazy that he got sacked.

آنقدر شکایت کردند که هیچکس دیگر گوش نداد. *ānqadr šekāyat kardand ke hickas digar guš nadād.* They complained so much that nobody listened any more.

دزد چنان تند دوید که زمین خورد. *dozd conān tond david ke zamin xord.* The thief ran so fast that he fell.

The verb in the result clause is in a non-subjunctive tense, because it expresses a fact.

9 . Clauses of time

See 8/4 above. Time clauses show when the action of the main verb takes or took place. The conjunctions introducing time clauses are best studied in groups:

- وقتیکه\وقتی که *vaqtike/vaqti ke* } when
  موقعیکه\موقعی که *mouqe'ike/mouqe'i ke* }

  بعد از اینکه *ba'd az inke* } after
  پس از اینکه *pas az inke* }

These conjunctions are usually followed by the past tense (5/8), irrespective of the timing. The time clause begins the sentence:

وقتی که خبر را شنیدیم تعجب کردیم.
vaqti ke xabar rā šenidim ta'ajjob kardim.
When we heard the news we were astonished.

موقعیکه علی رسید به من خبر بده*.* *mouqe'ike ali rasid*
be man xabar bedeh. When Ali arrives, tell me.

بعد از اینکه رفتید تلفن می‌کنم.
ba'd az inke raftid telefon mi konam.
After you have gone I shall telephone.

وقتی که ماشین آمد حرکت کردیم. *vaqti ke māšin āmad*
harakat kardim. When the car came/had come we set off.

* See 1/15. Final ه in this word is part of the root, and therefore not silent.

In terse statements in everyday speech, the conjunction is sometimes omitted from 'when' clauses:

ماشین آمد ، ما رفتیم. ‹*māšin umad, mā raftim.*›
The car comes, (and) we're off.

(See 5/9, second indent, for this use of the past tense in the main clause).

- از وقتیکه\از وقتی که *az vaqtike/az vaqti ke* since

After this conjunction the verb stands in the present tense (5/10). The time clause begins the sentence:

از وقتیکه اینجا کار می کنم اعتصابی نداشته ایم.

az vaqtike injā kār mi konam e'tesābi nadāšte im.

Since I have worked here we have had no strike(s).

- هر وقت (که) *har vaqt (ke)*
  هر موقع (که) *har mouqe' (ke)* } whenever

These conjunctions are followed either by the past tense, or by the imperfect tense (5/13) for repeated actions, regardless of the timing. The time clause begins the sentence:

هر وقت (که) او را دیدید به من بگویید. *har vaqt (ke)*

u rā didid be man beguid. Whenever you see him, tell me.

هر وقت (که) او را می‌دیدند می‌دویدند.

har vaqt (ke) u rā mi didand mi davidand.

Every time they saw him they used to run.

These conjunctions can also mean 'if ever' or 'if and when'; see 8/11.

- قبل از اینکه *qabl az inke*
  پیش از اینکه *piš az inke* } before

These conjunctions are followed by the subjunctive tense (5/16), irrespective of the timing. The time clause begins the sentence:

قبل از اینکه بروید این را امضا کنید. *qabl az inke*

beravid in rā emzā konid. Before you go, sign this.

قبل از اینکه برود این را امضا کرد. *qabl az inke*

beravad in rā emzā kard. Before he went he signed this.

- که *ke* when, as, as soon as

This conjunction is used in two ways:

- after the subject of the time clause. The subject must be stated, with a pronoun if necessary:

آنها که می‌رسند شروع می‌کنیم. *ānhā ke mi rasand*

šoru' mi konim. When they arrive we shall begin.

محمد که حاضر شد رفتند. *mohammad ke hāzer šod*

raftand. As soon as Mohammad was ready they went.

- heading the time clause when it follows the main clause,

especially when one action interrupts or overlaps another:

جلسه را شروع کرده بودیم که صدای سوت آتش
شنیده شد. *jalase rā šoru' karde budim ke sedāye sute
āteš šenide šod.* We had started the meeting when the
('noise of the') fire alarm was heard.

In a sentence of this kind, in Persian as in English, our attention focuses not on the main clause but on the time clause. This structure can also be seen in the last Persian example of 5/14.

- تا *tā* until/till; as long as

This conjunction is used in the following ways in time clauses:

- 'until/till': the time clause follows the main clause, and its verb stands in the subjunctive for present or future time and in the past tense for past time:

اینجا صبر کنید تا دکتر بیاید. *injā sabr konid tā doktor
biāyad ‹biād›.* Wait here until the doctor comes.

صبر کردم تا دکتر آمد. *sabr kardam tā doktor āmad.*
I waited till the doctor came.

- 'as long as': the time clause stands first:

تا اینجا کار می‌کنید این را فراموش نکنید.
tā injā kār mi konid in rā farāmuš nakonid.
As long as you work here, don't forget this.

10. Clauses of reason

See 8/4 above. Clauses of reason show why the main verb happens or happened. The introductory conjunctions for such clauses are:

برای اینکه *barāye inke*
زیراکه *zirā ke* } because
چون\چونکه *cun/cunke ‹con/conke›* as, since

159

براى اینکه *barāye inke* is by far the most common of these conjunctions in everyday Persian. It follows the main clause, as does زیراكه *zirā ke*. The conjunctions چون *cun* ‹con› and چونکه *cunke* ‹conke› can either begin the sentence or follow the main clause. The tense in the reason clause is that demanded by the meaning of the sentence:

نمى‌توانند بیایند براى اینکه مریضند. *nemi tavānand biāyand* ‹nemi tunand biānd› *barāye inke marizand.*
They can't come because they are ill.

چونکه مریض بودند نمى‌توانستند بیایند. *cunke* ‹conke› *mariz budand nemi tavānestand biāyand* ‹nemi tunestand biānd›.
As they were ill they couldn't come.

In speech, it is as common in Persian as it is in English to omit the main clause when answering a question asking چرا *cerā* 'why':

چرا کوشش نمى‌کنى؟ - براى اینکه نمى‌شود. *cerā kušeš nemi koni? - ‹ barāye inke nemi še.›*
Why don't you try? - Because it can't be done.

11. Conditional clauses

See 8/4 above. A conditional clause states subject to what condition the main clause is true. The conditional clause almost always begins the sentence.

We need to distinguish between *real* conditions, which are possible ('if it rains') and *unreal* conditions, which are impossible or at least unlikely ('if I had known').

Real conditions. Real conditions in present or future time are mostly introduced by one of the conjunctions

اگر *ágar* if   چنانچه *conānce* if

در صورتى که *dar surati ke* if, in case, in the event that

به شرطى که *be šarti ke* provided that

اگر *agar* is by far the commonest of these. The conditional clause has its verb in the subjunctive (5/16):

160

اگر باران ببارد منزل می‌مانیم. *agar bārān bebārad manzel mi mānim*. If it rains we'll stay at home.

اگر وقت داشته باشید*بفرمایید. *agar vaqt dāšte bāšid befarmāid*. If you have time, please (come).

به شرطی که به حسابداری خبر دهید می‌توانید ... *be šarti ke be hesābdāri xabar dehid ‹bedin›, mi tavānid ‹mi tunid› ...* Provided you inform Accounts, you can ...

در صورتی که حساب پرداخته نشود ما مبلغ ۲٪ ماهیانه اضافه می‌کنیم. *dar surati ke hesāb pardāxte našavad mā mablaqe do dar sad māhiāne ezāfe mi konim*. In the event that the bill is not paid we add ('a sum of') 2% per month ('monthly').

* for داشتن *dāštan* 'to have' the perfect subjunctive serves also as the (present) subjunctive; see 5/23.

In everyday Persian it is common also to use the past tense in the conditional clause of such sentences, when the condition is considered extremely likely:

اگر آنها‌را دیدید این بلیط‌را به آنها بدهید. *agar ānhā rā didid in bilit rā be ānhā bedehid*. If you see them give them this ticket.

اگر وقت نداشتید عیب ندارد. *agar vaqt nadāštid eib nadārad ‹nadāre›*. If you have no time, it does not matter.

In these two examples the 'if' almost means 'when'.

Real conditions in past time are rare. In these, the conditional clause has its verb in the perfect subjunctive; the verb of the main clause follows the logic of the sentence:

اگر قرارداد نرسیده باشد حتماً زنگ می‌زند. *agar qarārdād naraside bāšad ‹bāše› hatman zang mi zanad ‹mi zane›* If the contract has not arrived he will certainly ring.

اگر به شهر رفته باشد یادداشتی*نوشته است**. *agar be šahr rafte bāšad yāddāšti nevešte ast*. If he has gone to town he will have written a note.

* See 11/2 for the spelling of this word.

** Perfect tense with future-perfect meaning, see 5/22.

In a sentence such as the following, where the condition is known to be fulfilled already:

اگر مطمئن هستید بفرمایید. *agar motma'en hastid befarmāid.*
If/Since you're sure, go ahead.

the conditional verb can stand in the present tense (5/10). In such a sentence اگر means more 'since' than 'if' in English.

See also 8/9, Clauses of time, third indent. Clauses introduced by هر وقت (که) *har vaqt (ke),* هر موقع (که) *har mouqe' (ke)* can have a real conditional meaning, 'if ever ...' or 'if and when'. The verb goes into the past:

هر وقت (که) او را دیدید خبر بدهید. *har vaqt (ke) u rā didid*
xabar bedehid. If ever/If and when you see him, tell (me).

Unreal conditions. In both clauses of an unreal condition the verb stands in the imperfect tense (5/13; for داشتن *dāštan* 'to have' and بودن *budan* 'to be' the past tense, 5/8; the imperfect of شدن *šodan* 'to become' may also be preferred to the latter). The introductory conjunction is اگر *agar.* The time-sequence of the sentence sometimes has to be inferred from the context:

اگر آن را می‌دانستم به شما می‌گفتم. *agar ān rā mi dānestam*
be šomā mi goftam. If I knew that I would tell you.
or: If I had known that I would have told you.

اگر آن را باور می‌کردم خودم می‌رفتم. *agar ān rā bāvar*
mi kardam xodam mi raftam. If I believed that I would go myself.

اگر خودمان نمی‌دیدیم باور نمی‌کردیم.
agar xodemān ‹xodemun› nemi didim bāvar nemi kardim.
If we hadn't seen (it) ourselves we wouldn't have believed (it).

اگر یك نفر غایب بود\می‌شد می‌باختیم.
agar yek nafar qāyeb bud/mi šod mi bāxtim.
If one man had been absent we would have lost.

اگر رانندگان بیشتر توجه می‌کردند تصادمی نمی‌شد. *agar*
rānandegān bištar tavajjoh mi kardand tasādomi nemi šod. If the drivers had been more careful there would have been no collision.

In all conditions, the conjunction may often be dropped in everyday speech:

باران بیاید منزل می‌مانیم. ‹bārān biād manzel mi munim.›
Should it rain, we'll stay at home.

یك نفر غایب می‌شد ما می‌باختیم. yek nafar qāyeb mi šod mā
mi bāxtim. One man off and we'd have lost.

Negative conditions. 'Unless' is اگر agar with a negative verb, 'if
... not'; or مگر اینکه mágar inke with an affirmative verb and
following the main clause:

اگر عجله نکنید فایده ندارد. agar ajale nakonid fāyede nādārad
‹nadāre›. Unless you ('If you do not') hurry it will be useless.

فایده ندارد مگر اینکه عجله کنید. fāyede nādārad ‹nadāre›
magar inke ajale konid. It will be no good unless you hurry .

In English, 'if' can also be used to mean 'whether' in indirect
questions (8/3 above):

نمی‌دانم آیا می‌آید. nemi dānam āyā mi āyad
I do not know whether/if she is coming.

In Persian اگر 'if' is found only in conditional sentences.

'If not' is و اگرنه va agar ná (note the stress), which can be added
to any conditional sentence where it makes sense:

اگر حاضر باشد بیاید و اگرنه به من بگویید. agar hāzer bāšad
biāyad ‹bāše biād›, va agar na be man beguid ‹begid›.
If he is present, have him come (in); if not, tell me.

12. Clauses of concession

See 8/4 above. A clause of concession or concessive clause is the
opposite of a condition (8/11); it states *despite* or *irrespective of*
what circumstance the main clause is true. Clauses of concession
are introduced by one of the following conjunctions, the first four
meaning 'although', 'even though', 'even if':

با اینکه bā inke   با وجود اینکه bā vojude inke

اگرهم\اگر...هم ágarham /ágar...ham   اگرچه ágarce (NB stress)

and   هرچه har ce however (much)

The concessive clause usually begins the sentence, and its verb

163

stands in the tense demanded by the time-sequence:

با اینکه فقیر است شکایت نمی‌کند. *bā inke faqir ast šekāyat*
nemi konad. Although he is poor he does not complain.

اگر رئیس هم عددهارا قبول کرده است من می‌خواهم دوباره
نگاه کنم. *agar rais ham adadhā rā qabul karde ast man*
mi xāham dobāre negāh konam. Even though the boss
has accepted the figures, I want to look again.

هرچه کوشش می کنید نمی‌شود.
har ce kušeš mi konid nemi šavad ‹nemi še›.
However (much) you try it won't work ('won't become').

اگرچه *ágarce* is commoner in writing than in speech. When it is
used, the main clause is usually introduced by اما *ámmā* or ولی
váli, both meaning 'but', yet probably best translated here (if
translated at all) as 'nevertheless':

اگرچه وزیر برگشته است ولی تصمیمی اعلام نشده است.
agarce vazir bar gašte ast vali tasmimi e'lām našode ast.
Although the minister has returned, ('nevertheless')
no decision has been announced.

جلفا، کلیسای وانک *jolfā - kalisāye vānk* Julfa -
The Armenian ('Vank') Cathedral

13. Clauses of manner

See 8/4 above. Clauses of manner show how or in what manner the main verb takes place. The commonest introductory conjunction for such a clause is

مثل اینکه *mesle inke* as if, as though

صحبت می‌کرد مثل اینکه مرا خوب می‌شناخت.

sohbat mi kard mesle inke marā xub mi šenāxt.
He/She spoke as if he/she knew me well.

‹پیاده می‌رود مثل اینکه مست است. ‹*piāde mi re mesle inke*
mast e.› He walks as if he is/were drunk.

14. Topic and comment

Examine the sentences

پسر همسایهٔ جدید من پزشك است.

pesare hamsāyeye jadide man pezešk ast.
My new neighbour's son is a doctor.

همسایهٔ جدید من و پسرش را دیده اید؟

hamsāyeye jadide man o pesareš rā dide id?
Have you seen my new neighbour and his son?

These are technically correct as they stand; but they are more natural as

همسایهٔ جدید من ، پسرش پزشك است.

hamsāyeye jadide man, pesareš pezešk ast.
'My new neighbour, his son is a doctor.'

همسایهٔ جدید من و پسر او، آنها را دیده اید؟

hamsāyeye jadide man o pesare u, ānhā rā dide id?
'My new neighbour and his son, have you seen them?'

When the subject or object of the sentence is a complex expression, it is common, even in written Persian, to break the sentence and restate the subject or object with a pronoun (4/2, 3) or a possessive adjective (3/11), as shown above. This structure can be called 'topic and comment'. The written comma between the first part (the topic) and the second (the comment) may sometimes be absent from the Persian text, but there is always a short pause in pronunciation.

We have topic and comment in English, but only in everyday speech:

> Last night's cello soloist, wasn't he a bit flamboyant?

Topic and comment is especially useful in the quasi-impersonal structures described in 8/15 below.

15. Quasi-impersonal structures

Certain expressions of mood can be made with quasi-impersonal expressions in Persian.

Liking and disliking. In addition to the compound verb دوست داشتن دار... *dust dāštan dār-* 'to like' which is used with a personal subject:

این مشروب را دوست (نـ)دارم. *in mašrub rā dust (na)dāram.*
I (don't) like this drink.

we have the quasi-impersonal or reversed structures

از ... خوشـ... آمدن *az ... xoš... āmadan* (for 'liking')
از ... بد... آمدن *az ... bad... āmadan* (for 'disliking')

The structures are best understood by studying examples:

از این مشروب خوشم (نـ)می آید. *az in mašrub xošam (ne)mi āyad.* I (don't) like this drink.

از دیدن انها همیشه بدش می آمد. *az didane ānhā hamiše badeš mi āmad.* He always disliked seeing them.

از دیدن اعضای کمیته همیشه بدش می آمد. *az didane a'zāye komite hamiše badeš mi āmad.* He always disliked seeing (the) members of the committee.

Note:

- The thing liked or disliked is put after the preposition از *az* 'from'. It can be a pronoun, a noun or any expression equivalent to a noun (such as a long infinitive with its object, see 5/2).
- The structure is not completely impersonal, since it has an

identified subject, which is either خوش *xoš* or بد *bad*, with the appropriate tense of ...آ آمدن *āmadan ā-* in the 3rd person singular.

- The person who likes or dislikes is expressed as a possessive suffix attached to خوش *xoš* or بد *bad*.

The examples given above express the person as a pronoun. When we wish to express the person as a noun, we use 'topic and comment' (8/14 above) to restate it, i.e. putting the noun or noun expression first and reflecting it in the possessive suffix attached to خوش or بد :

اعضای کمیته از دیدن او خوششان نخواهد آمد.

a'zāye komite az didane u xošešān naxāhad āmad.
The committee members won't like seeing him.
('The committee members, they won't like seeing him.')

Feeling sleepy; falling asleep. These are also best expressed quasi-impersonally:

خوابش آمده (است). ‹xābeš umade (ast)› He/She feels sleepy.

خوابش برد. *xābeš bord.* He/She fell asleep.

These have a pronoun as the affected party. To re-express with a noun, we use 'topic and comment' as shown above:

بچه ها خوابشان آمده است. *baccehā, xābešān āmade ast.* The children are feeling sleepy. ('The children, their sleep has come.')

بچه خوابش برده است. *bacce, xābeš borde ast.*
The baby's fallen asleep.

See 1/13 for the pronunciation of خوش *xoš* and جواب *xāb*.

16. Wishes and exclamations

Wishes are most commonly introduced with کاش که *kāš ke* 'Would that'. The verb goes into the subjunctive (5/16) if the wish is still realisable, and into the imperfect or pluperfect tense (5/13, 25) if the wish can no longer be realised:

کاش که بیایید! *kāš ke biāid!* I wish you would come!

کاش که می‌آمدی\آمده بودی! *kāš ke mi āmadi/āmade budi!*
I wish you had come!

'How ...' and 'What ...' in exclamations are expressed with چه *ce* before an indefinite noun (3/2, 8), an adjective (3/6) or an adverb (7/1):

چه خانهٔ بزرگی. *ce xāneye bozorgi.* What a big house.

چه قشنگ (است)! *ce qašang (‹e›)!* How beautiful (it is)!

چه خوب بازی می‌کنند. *ce xub bāzi mi konand.*
How well they play.

9. Numbers

1. Numerals

The numerals are:

۱ 1	۲ 2	۳ 3	٤\۴ 4	٥\۵ 5
٦\۶ 6	۷ 7	۸ 8	۹ 9	۰ 0

You will note that numerals 4, 5 and 6 have alternative forms.

2. Cardinal Numbers

Cardinal numbers ('one', 'two') express quantity and are used in counting. They are shown below (with colloquial pronunciation in angular quotation marks ‹ ›). The numerals in compound numbers are written from left to right →:

۰	0	صفر *sefr*				
۱	1	یك *yek*	۲	2	دو *do*	
۳	3	سه *se*	۴	4	چهار *cahār* ‹cār›	
۵	5	پنج *panj*	۶	6	شش *šeš*	
۷	7	هفت *haft*	۸	8	هشت *hašt*	
۹	9	نه *noh*	۱۰	10	ده *dah*	
۱۱	11	یازده *yāzdah*	۱۲	12	دوازده *davāzdah*	
۱۳	13	سیزده *sizdah*	۱۴	14	چهارده *cahārdah*	
۱۵	15	پانزده *pānzdah* ‹punzdah›	۱۶	16	شانزده *šānzdah* ‹šunzdah›	
۱۷	17	هوده *hevdah/hivdah*	۱۸	18	هجده\هیجده *hejdah/hijdah* ‹heždah/hiždah›	
۱۹	19	نوزده *nuzdah*	۲۰	20	بیست *bist*	
۲۱	21	بیست و یك *bist o yek*	۲۲	22	بیست و دو *bist o do*	
۳۰	30	سی *si*	۴۰	40	چهل *cehel*	
۵۰	50	پنجاه *panjāh*	۶۰	60	شصت *šast*	
۷۰	70	هفتاد *haftād*	۸۰	80	هشتاد *haštād*	
۹۰	90	نود *navad*	۱۰۰	100	صد *sad*	

۱۰۵	105	صد و پنج	*sad o panj*
۱۳۰	130	صد و سی	*sad o si*
۱۶۴	164	صد و شصت و چهار	*sad o šast o cahār*
۲۰۰	200	دویست	*devist*
۲۵۹	259	دویست و پنجاه و نه	*devist o panjāh o noh*
۳۰۰	300	سیصد	*sisad*
۴۰۰	400	چهارصد	*cahār sad*
۵۰۰	500	پانصد ‹punsad›	*pānsad* ‹punsad›
۶۰۰	600	ششصد\شش صد	*šessad/šeš sad*
۷۰۰	700	هفتصد\هفت صد	*haftsad/haft sad*
۸۰۰	800	هشتصد\هشت صد	*haštsad/hašt sad*
۹۰۰	900	نهصد\نه صد	*nohsad/noh sad*
۱۰۰۰	1000	هزار	*hezār*
۲۰۰۰	2000	دو هزار	*do hezār*
۳۰۰۰	3000	سه هزار	*se hezār*
۴۰۰۰	4000	چهار هزار	*cahār hezār*
۵۰۰۰	5000	پنجهزار\پنج هزار	*panjhezār/panj hezār*
۶۰۰۰	6000	ششهزار\شش هزار	*šešhezār/šeš hezār*
۷۰۰۰	7000	هفتهزار\هفت هزار	*hafthezār/haft hezār*
۸۰۰۰	8000	هشتهزار\هشت هزار	*hašthezār/hašt hezār*
۹۰۰۰	9000	نه هزار	*noh hezār*
۱۰۰۰۰۰۰	1,000,000	ملیون	*melyun*
۲۰۰۰۰۰۰	2,000,000	دو ملیون	*do melyun*

Note:

- After a number, the counted noun is always in the singular:

  دوازده ساعت *davāzdah sā'at* twelve hours

- The form يك *yek* 'one' is used in counting, or with a counted noun. Used otherwise, it mostly takes the form یکی *yeki*:

  یک شخص هست. *yek šaxs hast.* There is one person.

  but: یکی هست. *yeki hast.* There is one.

- With a counted noun denoting people, it is common to add نفر *nafar* 'person(s)' after the number; with a counted noun

170

denoting objects, it is common to add تا *tā* 'pieces' after the number:

صد نفر سرباز *sad nafar sarbāz* a hundred soldiers

شش تا مداد جدید *šeš tā medāde jadid* six new pencils

In everyday Persian تا *tā* is commonly used also for people.

- Although the counted noun is singular in form, an expression indicating two or more has a plural verb:

سه نفر مهندس گزارش دادند. *se nafar mohandes gozāreš dādand.* Three engineers reported.

- Compound numbers run from greatest to smallest, all elements being connected with و pronounced *o* 'and':

هزار و دویست و سی و پنج *hezār o devist o si o panj* one thousand two hundred and thirty-five

- The highest number used with صد *sad* 'hundred' is نه *noh* 'nine'; we must therefore express a number like 'twelve hundred' as هزار و دویست *hezār o devist* 'one thousand two hundred'.

- صد *sad* 'hundred', هزار *hezār* 'thousand' and ملیون *melyun* 'million' are preceded by یك *yek* 'one' only when 'one' is emphasised:

فقط یك ملیون *faqat yek melyun* only one million

These words are also nouns, and can be made plural:

چند نفر آمدند؟ – هزرها. *cand nafar āmadand?* - *hezarhā.* How many people came? - Thousands.

The *ezāfe* (3/5) is not used in plural expressions such as:

صدها نفر رفتند. *sadhā nafar raftand.* Hundreds ('of people') went.

- The numbers are indefinite in meaning as they stand. They can be made definite by adding an adjective with definite meaning, e.g. a demonstrative such as این *in* 'this' or آن *ān* 'that' (3/12) or a definite distributive such as هر *har* 'every' (3/14):

171

سه تا کتاب خریدم. ‏ *se tā ketāb xaridam.*
I bought three books.

آن سه تا گرانند. ‏ *ān se tā gerānand.*
Those three are expensive.

همین سه تا کتاب را خریدید؟ ‏ *hamin se tā ketāb rā*
xaridid? Did you buy the same three books?

هر سه افسر تقصیر دارند. ‏ *har se afsar taqsir dārand.*
All three officers are to blame ('have blame').

هر دو دانشجو امتحان دادند. ‏ *har do dānešju emtehān*
dādand. Both students took an examination.

And note هر دوشان ‏ *har doešān* 'both of them', with the
possessive suffix (3/11).

3. Ordinal numbers

Ordinal numbers ('first', 'second') show a place in a sequence. The
first three ordinal numbers are irregular:

اوّل ‏ *avvál* first   دوّم ‏ *dovvóm* second   سوّم ‏ *sevvóm* third

All others are regularly formed by adding the stressed suffix م...
-óm to the cardinal number. '-first' in compound numbers is یکم
yekom. The ordinal number in these forms is a definite adjective
which follows its noun (if there is one) after an *ezāfe* (3/8):

پانزدهم ‏ *pānzdahom* ‹*punzdahom*› (the) fifteenth
روز اوّل ‏ *ruze avval* the first day

قرن بیست و یکم ‏ *qarne bist o yekom* the twenty-first century

Persian often uses the ordinal number where English prefers the
cardinal:

درس ششم را خواندیم. ‏ *darse šešom rā xāndim.*
We read Lesson 6 ('the sixth lesson').

Another form of the ordinal number is made by attaching ین... *-ín*
(stressed) to the form shown above. This form is used like a
superlative adjective (3/10), i.e preceding the noun, with no *ezāfe*;
or like a pronoun, i.e. with no noun:

اولین دانشجو *avvalin dānešju* the first student

چهاردهمین هفتهٔ سال *cahārdahomin hafteye sāl*
the fourteenth week of the year

این دهمین است. *in dahomin ast ‹e›.* This is the tenth (one).

4. Other numerical expressions

Other expressions of number or numerical order deserve attention:

- Once, twice (etc.) are expressed with words such as مرتبه *martabe,* بار *bār* or دفعه *daf'e,* all meaning 'a time':

یك مرتبه\بار\دفعه *yek martabe/bār/daf'e* once

صد مرتبه\بار\دفعه *sad martabe/bār/daf'e* a hundred times

روزی سه مرتبه *ruzi se martabe* three times daily

and note: چند مرتبه\بار\دفعه *cand martabe/bār/daf'e* a few times

چند مرتبه\بار\دفعه؟ *cand martabe/bār/daf'e?* how many times?

- 'Or' is not expressed in approximations like the following:

ده پانزده *dah pānzdah ‹punzdah›* ten or fifteen

- Distributive and repetitive numbers:

یکی یکی *yeki yeki* singly, one by one

but: دو تا دو تا *do tā do tā* (NB stress) two by two

ده تا ده تا *dah tā dah tā* ten at a time

سه روز به سه روز *se ruz be se ruz* every three days

- '-odd': سی و اند *si o and* thirty-odd

- چندم *candóm* and چندمین *candomín,* used in questions, preceding the noun; چندم *candom* is followed by *ezāfe* (3/8), چندمین *candomin* is not, but its noun has indefinite ی... *-i* (3/2):

امروز چندم ماه است؟ *emruz candome māh ast ‹e›?*
What day ('the how-manyeth') of the month is it today?

این چندمین مرتبه‌ای است که گفتم ...؟ *in candomin martabei st ke goftam ...?* How many times have I said ...?
('This is the how-manyeth time that I have said ...?')

چندم and چندمین are not directly translatable into English. They are the exact equivalent of German 'der/die/das wievielte'.

5 . Fractions and percentage

Fractions. 'half' is نیم *nim,* used directly before the noun:

نیم ساعت *nim sā'at* half an hour

'and a half' is و نیم *o nim,* after the counted noun:

دو سال و نیم *do sāl o nim* two and a half years

Ordinal numbers (9/3 above) from سوم *sevvom* 'third' upwards are also used as fractions:

$\frac{2}{3}$\ دو سوم وزن *do sevvome vazn* $^2/_3$ of the weight

یك پنجم *yek panjom* one fifth

نه دهمش *noh dahomeš* nine tenths of it

We also commonly use the Arabic fractions for 'half' to 'fifth':

نصف *nesf* half   ثلث *sols* third

ربع *rob'/rob* quarter   خمس *xoms* fifth

دو ثلث *do sols* two thirds

سه ربع *se rob'/rob* three quarters

Percentage. There are two ways of expressing percentage:

شصت در صد \ ٪٦٠ \ *šast dar sad* 60%

or, less common: اصدی دوازده \ ٪١٢ \ *sadi davāzdah* 12%

6 . Other adjectival forms, and adverbial forms

Adjectival forms. Adjectives are formed from some numerical expressions by adding -*é* (stressed) + silent final ه (1/15):

برنامهٔ پنجساله *barnāmeye panjsālé* the five-year programme

مذاکره ای چهارروزه *mozākerei cahārruze* a four-day conference

ماشین دونفره *māšine donafare* a/the two-seater car

روابط دوطرفه *ravābete dotarafe* bilateral relations

بچهٔ هشت سالهای *bacceye hašt sālei* an eight-year-old child

If the counted noun already ends in silent ه, this becomes گی... -*gí*

174

(also stressed on the -*í*):

معالجه‌ای سه هفتگی *mo'ālejei se haftegí* a three-week treatment

Adverbial forms. For the adverbial forms 'first(ly)', 'second(ly)' etc., used to enumerate items, Persian uses the Arabic adverbs. We need to know only the first five. Note the final stress:

اولاً *avvalán* first(ly)   ثانیاً *sānián* second(ly)

ثالثاً *sālesán* third(ly)   رابعاً *rābe'án* fourth(ly)

خامساً *xāmesán* fifth(ly)

دو تا عدد لازم داریم، اولاً قیمت و ثانیاً خرج بیمه. *do tā adad lāzem dārim, avvalan qeimat va sānian xarje bime.* We need two figures; first, the price, and second, the cost of insurance.

7 . ابجد *abjad*

In English we frequently use alphabetical letters or Roman numerals to number parts of a document. In Persian, this is done with alphabetical letters. Every letter of the alphabet has a numerical value for this purpose; we need to know only the values of the first ten, which are:

ابجد هوز حطی

10 9 8 7 6 5 4 3 2 1

for which a simple memory aid is used: *abjad havvaz hoti.*

ا. مقدمه *alef. moqaddame*   (a)/(i) Introduction

ب. عمومیات *be. omumiyāt*   (b)/(ii) General ('Generalities')

ج. وضعیت مالی *jim. vaz'iyate māli*   (c)/(iii) Financial Situation

8 . Measurement

We do not use the *ezāfe* (3/5) with units of measurement:

دو کیلو و نیم شکر *do kilou o nim šakar* two and a half kilos of sugar

سه فنجان چای *se fenjān ‹fenjun› cāi* three cups of tea

ده لیتر آب *dah litr āb* ten litres of water

دو جفت جوراب *do joft jurāb* two pairs of socks

Dimensions and weights are expressed so:

اندازهٔ این میز چقدر است ‹e›؟ *andāzeye in miz ceqadr ast ‹e›?* What does this table measure ('How much is the measurement of ...')?

اندازه‌اش دو متر در یك متر و هشتاد است.
andāzeaš do metr dar yek metr o haštād ast ‹e›.
It measures two metres by one metre eighty.

طولش یك متر و نیم و عرضش نود سانتیمتر. *tuleš yek metr o nim va arzeš navad sāntimetr.* It (is) one and a half metres long and ninety centimetres wide ('Its length ... and its width ...').

قطعه ای به مساحت ده هكتار *qet'ei be mesāhate dah hektār* a plot measuring ten hectares ('to the area of ...')

وزن این بسته چقدر است ‹e›؟ *vazne in baste ceqadr ast ‹e›?* How heavy is ('What is the weight of') this parcel?

وزنش چهار كیلو و دویست گرم. *vazneš cahār kilou o devist gram.* It weighs four kilos and two hundred grams.

برادرم هشتاد كیلو وزن دارد.
barādaram haštād kilou vazn dārad ‹dāre›.
My brother weighs eighty kilos ('has eighty kilos weight').

9 . Calculation

Calculations are most commonly expressed with می‌شود *mi šavad* (colloquially, ‹mi še›) 'becomes', in the middle of the expression:

شش و چهار می‌شود ده. *šeš o cahār mi šavad dah.*
Six plus four makes ten.

پنج از نه می‌شود چهار. *panj az noh mi šavad cahār.*
Five from nine leaves four.

هشت چهار تا می‌شود سی و دو. *hašt cahār tā mi šavad si o do.*
Eight times four is thirty-two.

هفت تقسیم بر دو می‌شود سه و نیم. *haft taqsim bar do mi šavad se o nim.* Seven divided by two is three and a half.

10 . Clock

Important vocabulary for telling the time:

ساعت *sā'at* hour, clock, watch   دقیقه *daqiqe* minute

ثانیه *sānie* (a) second   نیم *nim* half

ربع *rob'/rob* quarter   و *o* ('and') past

به *be* to   کم *kam* (here) less, minus

صبح *sobh* morning   ظهر *zohr* noon, midday

بعد از ظهر *ba'd az zohr* afternoon   عصر *asr* evening

شب *šab* night   نصف شب *nesfe šab* midnight

ساعت چند است؟ *sā'at cand ast ‹e›?* What time is it?

Examples:

ساعت یک\دو است. *sā'ate yek/do ast.* It is one/two o'clock.

(ساعت) سه و نیم *(sā'ate) se o nim* half past three

(ساعت) چهار و ربع *(sā'ate) cahār o rob'/rob*
       a quarter past four

(ساعت) چهار و پانزده دقیقه *(sā'ate) cahār o pānzdah daqiqe*
       fifteen minutes past four

(ساعت) پنج و ده دقیقه *(sā'ate) panj o dah daqiqe*
       ten past five

(ساعت) شش و دوازده دقیقه *(sā'ate) šeš o davāzdah daqiqe*
       twelve minutes past six

یک ربع به هفت *yek rob'/rob be haft*

(ساعت) هفت یک ربع کم *(sā'ate) haft yek rob'/rob kam* }
       a quarter to seven

بیست دقیقه به هشت *bist daqiqe be hašt*

(ساعت) هشت بیست دقیقه کم *(sā'ate) hašt bist daqiqe kam* }
       twenty to eight

You will note from these examples:

- For time on the hour, the word ساعت must be used. Everywhere else it can be dropped.

- The word دقیقه is always present other than on the full hour, the half and the quarters.

- For time from the hour to half-past there is only one common formula. For time from the half-hour to the next hour, there are two formulæ.

11.   Calendar

Three calendars are used in Iran.

The official Iranian calendar. This calendar, called سال هجری
خورشیدی *sāle hejriye xoršidi* 'the solar hejri year', is used for all
official and national purposes:

month		days	western date of first day
فروردین ١	*farvardin*	31	(Spring equinox) 21 or 22 March
اردیبهشت ٢	*ordibehešt*	31	
خرداد ٣	*xordād*	31	
تیر ۴	*tir*	31	(Summer solstice) 21 or 22 June
مرداد ۵	*mordād*	31	
شهریور ۶	*šahrivar*	31	
مهر ٧	*mehr*	30	(Autumn equinox) 21 or 22 Sept.
آبان ٨	*ābān*	30	
آذر ٩	*āzar*	30	
دی ١٠	*dei*	30	(Winter solstice) 21 or 22 Dec.
بهمن ١١	*bahman*	30	
اسفند ١٢	*esfand*	29; 30 in a leap year	

Each of these names may be followed by ماه... *-māh* 'month'; this is
commoner with the shorter names, e.g. تیرماه *tirmāh*.

The international or western calendar. This calendar year is
known as سال میلادی *sāle milādi* 'the Christian year', and is used
for international relations and trade. The months are pronounced
in imitation of the French from which they are taken:

ژانویه *žānvié* January		فوریه *fevrié* February	
مارس *mārs* March		آوریل *āvríl* April	
مه *me* May		ژوئن *žuán* June	
ژوئیه *žuié* July		اوت *ut* August	
سپتامبر *septámber* September		اکتبر *október* October	
نوامبر *novámber* November		دسامبر *desámber* December	

1 January 2000 AD corresponded to 11 Dei 1378 AH Iranian.

(AH is Anno Hegiræ, the Year of the Flight.)

The Moslem calendar. This has a lunar year, سال هجری قمری
sāle hejriye qamari 'the lunar hejri year'. It has twelve months and
lasts 354 or 355 days; the year count dates from the Prophet
Mohammad's flight from Mecca to Medina in 622 AD. It is used to
mark Moslem religious events:

محرم	١	*mohárram*	30 days
صفر	٢	*sáfar*	30
ربیع الاول	٣	*rabí'ol'avvál*	30
ربیع الثانی	۴	*rabí'ossáni*	30
جمادی الاولی	۵	*jomādal'úla*	30
جمادی الاخری	۶	*jomādal'óxra*	30
رجب	٧	*rájab*	29
شعبان	٨	*ša'bán*	29
رمضان	٩	*ramazán*	29
شوال	١٠	*šavvál*	29
ذوالقعده	١١	*zolqá'de*	29
ذوالحجه	١٢	*zolhéjje*	29 or 30

Newspapers usually carry all three dates.

The days of the week are:

جمعه *jom'e* Friday　　　　　شنبه *šambe* Saturday

یکشنبه *yekšambe* Sunday　　دوشنبه *došambe* Monday

سه شنبه *sešambe* Tuesday　چهارشنبه *cahāršambe* Wednesday

پنجشنبه *panjšambe* Thursday

These names are often preceded by روز *ruz* 'day' with the *ezáfe*
(3/5): روزشنبه *ruze šambe*.

Traditionally, the day starts at sunset. Care is therefore needed
with expressions such as:

شب (روز) جمعه *šabe (ruze) jom'e* Thursday night

شب شنبه *šabe šambe* Friday night

but: (روز) جمعه شب *(ruze) jom'e šab* Friday night

179

Dates. We express dates with the ordinal numbers, as in English:

۱۳۷۹\۳\۱۰ خ؛ (روز) چهارشنبه دهم خرداد(ماه) سال هزار

و سیصد و هفتاد و نه خورشیدی *(ruze) cahāršambe dahome*
xordād(māh)e sāle hezār o sisad o haftād o nohe xoršidi
Wednesday 10th Khordad ('of') 1379 AH Iranian

۱۹۹۹\۱۲\۳۱ م؛ (روز) جمعه سی و یکم دسامبر سال هزار و

نه صد و نود و نه میلادی *(ruze) jom'e si o yekome desāmbere*
sāle hezār o noh sad o navad o nohe milādi
Friday 31st December ('of') 1999 AD

12. Age

A person's age (سِنّ *sen*) is expressed as follows:

سنش چقدر است؟ *senneš ceqadr ast ‹e›?* } How old is
چند سال دارد؟ *cand sāl dārad ‹dāre›?* } he/she?

سنش بیست سال است. *senneš bist sāl ast ‹e›.* } He/She is
بیست سال دارد. *bist sāl dārad ‹dāre›.* } 20 years old.

اصفهان، کاخ چهل ستون *esfahān - kāxe cehel sotun*
Isfahan - Palace of Chehel Sotun ('Forty Pillars')

10. Arabic Forms

1. General

The whole grammar and most basic vocabulary of Persian are Indo-European. But much abstract vocabulary has been taken from Arabic and is commonly used, having survived various language reforms in Iran. This Arabic vocabulary mostly keeps its Arabic spelling, but is pronounced in a Persian manner; often also the meaning is different. This book shows the Persian pronunciation and meaning; and the Persian spelling where it is different..

It used to be common to learn substantial parts of Arabic grammar as part of Persian language studies. This is not necessary; it suffices to learn a few Arabic forms for recognition. It is no more important to know Arabic thoroughly for studying Persian than it is, for example, to know French for studying English.

Arabic plurals of nouns are examined in 3/4.

2. Participles

Chapter 5/20 gives a definition of a participle and shows how Persian present and past participles are formed and used.

Arabic also has participles formed from its own verbs. Persian uses these participles as nouns (mostly denoting a person) or as adjectives.

Common patterns:

-ā-e-:

تاجر *tājer* merchant   شامل *šāmel* including

باعث *bā'es/bāes* cause   نایب *nāyeb* deputy, lieutenant

حاکم *hākem* governor   سابق *sābeq* former, preceding

-a-ā-, -a-ā:

نجار *najjār* carpenter   نقاش *naqqāš* painter

بنا *bannā* builder

ma-u-:

مشروب *mašrub* drink   منشور *manšur* decree, diploma

ممنون *mamnun* grateful   ممنوع *mamnu'* forbidden

مخصوص *maxsus* special   مقصود *maqsud* purpose

معروف *ma'ruf* well-known   محسوب *mahsub* billed

مسئول *mas'ul* responsible

mo-e-:

معلم *mo'allem* teacher   (معرفى *mo'arrefí* presentation)

مفسر *mofasser* commentator   مسافر *mosāfer* traveller

مناسب *monāseb* suitable   مواظب *movāzeb* careful

ممكن *momken* possible   مشكل *moškel* difficult

مضحك *mozhek* funny   مهمّ *mohem* important

مؤمن *mo'men* believer   متشكر *motašakker* grateful

متمدن *motamadden* civilised   متوجه* *motavajjeh* attentive

متخصص *motaxasses* expert   متأسف\متاسف *mota(')assef* sorry

مختلف *moxtalef* various   محتمل *mohtamel* probable

مفتخر *moftaxer* proud   منتظر *montazer* awaiting

* See 1/15. This final ه is part of the root, and is pronounced *h*.

mo-a-, mo-ā-:

مصمم *mosammam* decided   محترم *mohtaram* respected

مقدس *moqaddas* sacred   مشرف *mošarraf* honoured

مرتب *morattab* arranged, regular   منظم *monazzam* orderly

(مجدداً *mojaddadan* afresh)   موفق *movaffaq* successful

مطلق *motlaq* absolute   مثبت *mosbat* positive

معتمد *mo'tamad* trusted   منتخب *montaxab* elected

مختصر *moxtasar* abbreviated   محتاج *mohtāj* needy

mo-i-, mo-i:

مدير *modir* director   مفيد *mofid* useful

منشى *monši* clerk   مبتدى *mobtadi* beginner

Note:

- Many of these participles can be given appropriate Persian prefixes or suffixes, or incorporated into Persian compounds, or extended with Arabic endings used in Persian:

مسئولیت *mas'uliyat* responsibility

معلمین\معلمان\معلمها
mo'allemin/mo'allemān/mo'allemhā teachers

مفیدتر *mofidtar* more useful

نقاشی *naqqāši* (profession/activity of) painting

محسوب کردن *mahsub kardan* to place on account

معرفی کردن *mo'arrefí kardan* to introduce, present

and some of them (shown in parentheses above) are used only with an ending (Arabic or Persian) added:

معرفی *mo'arrefí* presentation

مجدداً *mojaddadan* afresh

- Since the participles are used as nouns or adjectives, they often occur as complement (see 5/6) of verbs such as بودن باش... *budan bāš-* 'to be' or شدن شو... *šodan šav-* 'to become':

خیلی متأسفم. *xeili mota'assefam.* I am very sorry.

مواظب باشید. *movāzeb bāšid.* Be careful.

ناگهان مسئله مهمتر شد. *nāgahān masale mohemtar šod.*
Suddenly the problem became more important.

3. Verbal nouns

An Arabic verbal noun usually denotes the activity or result of the verb from which it is derived. Common patterns found in such words used in Persian:

ta-i-, *tou-i-*:

تصمیم *tasmim* decision	تشکیل *taškil* formation
تعطیل *ta'til* holiday	تعمیر *ta'mir* repair
تغییر *taqyir* change	تشریف *tašrif* honouring
تسلیم *taslim* submission	ترتیب *tartib* arrangement
تأسیس *ta'sis* founding	تجدید *tajdid* renewal

183

تدبیر *tadbir* plan   تحویل *tahvil* transfer

تدریج *tadrij* gradation   تدریس *tadris* tuition

تعلیم *ta'lim* teaching   تقسیم *taqsim* dividing

تمرینٍ *tamrin* exercise   تقصیر *taqsir* fault, defect

(تقریباً *taqriban* approximately)   تنبیه *tambih* punishment

تألیف *ta'lif* (artistic) composition

تولید *toulid* production   توقیف *touqif* arrest

ta-e-e, ta-iye, ta-iyat:

تجربه *tajrebe* experience   تصفیه *tasfiye* refining

تربیت *tarbiyat* education

ta-o-:

تأسف *ta(')assof* regret   تصادف *tasādof* coincidence

تصور *tasavvor* imagination   تمدن *tamaddon* civilisation

توجه *tavajjoh* attention   تعجب *ta'ajjob* surprise

mo-ā-e-e, mo-ā-e-at:

معامله *mo'āmele* transaction   محافظه *mohāfeze* conservation

مخابره *moxābere* message   مشاهده *mošāhede* observation

مذاکره *mozākere* conference   معالجه *mo'āleje* (medical) treatment

مساعده *mosā'ede* advance (money)

مراجعت *morāje'at* return   مسافرت *mosāferat* journey

e-ā-, e-ā, e-ā-e, e-ā-at:

احترام *ehterām* respect   ابتدا *ebtedā* beginning

اتفاق *ettefāq* event   اتحاد *ettehād* union

اختیار *extiār* choice   اجبار *ejbār* compulsion

اهتمام *ehtemām* care   انقلاب *enqelāb* revolution

انحراف *enherāf* diversion   انتخاب *entexāb* (s)election

انتقاد *enteqād* criticism   امکان *emkān* possibility

التفات *eltefāt* kindness   اقدام *eqdām* measure, action

اقتصاد *eqtesād* economy   افتخار *eftexār* honour, pride

اعتماد *e'temād* confidence   اصلاح *eslāh* reform

اشتباه *eštebāh* mistake   اسلام *eslām* Islam

استثنا *estesnā* exception   ازدواج *ezdevāj* marriage

ارسال *ersāl* despatch(ing)   اجازه *ejāze* permission

اضافه *ezāfe* addition   ادامه *edāme* continuation

اداره *edāre* administration   استفاده *estefāde* utilisation, profit

اراده *erāde* will, wish   ارادت *erādat* sincerity

اقامت *eqāmat* stay   اشارت *ešārat* sign, signal

Note:

- Many of these verbal nouns can be given appropriate Persian prefixes or suffixes, or incorporated into Persian compounds, or extended with Arabic endings used in Persian:

اداری *edāri* administrative

انقلابی *enqelābi* revolutionary

تصمیمش *tasmimeš* his/her decision

تصادفاً *tasādofan* coincidentally

اتفاقاً *ettefāqan* by chance

ارادتمند *erādatmand* sincere

تصفیه‌خانه *tasfiyexāne* refinery

and some of them (one is shown in parentheses above) are more commonly used with an ending (Arabic or Persian) added:

تقریباً *taqriban* approximately

- The verbal nouns make a multitude of compound verbs (see 5/29). Many of these are formed with کن... کردن *kardan kon-*, often having passive forms (5/30) with شو... شدن *šodan šav-*:

تعمیر کردن\شدن *ta'mir kardan/šodan*
to repair/be repaired

انتخاب کردن\شدن *entexāb kardan/šodan*
to choose/be chosen

تعجب کردن *ta'ajjob kardan* to be astonished

اجازه دادن *ejāze dādan* to permit

- For the endings -*e* and -*at*, see 10/4 below.
- Some Arabic verbal nouns used in Persian have no regular pattern; they are also used in the manners described above:

عمل *amal*
practice, operation

عملى *amali*
practical, operative

قرار *qarār*
settlement, rest

قرارداد *qarārdād*
contract

بيقرار *biqarār* restless

قرار گرفتن گیر... *qarār gereftan gir-* to become settled

4. Word-ending ة... -*a*/-*at*

Many Arabic nouns (including some verbal nouns, see 10/3 above) have the ending ة... in their original language. This mixed letter consists of ه *he* with the dots of ت *te*, and is pronounced in Arabic sometimes as -*a*, sometimes as -*at*.

When such nouns are used in Persian, the ending becomes in some examples ه... -*e* (with silent ه , 1/15), and in others ت... -*at*:

ملاحظه *molāheze* regard

مدرسه *madrase* school

اضافه *ezāfe* addition

نتیجه *natije* result

ملت *mellat* nation

قاعده *qā'ede* rule

مسافرت *mosāferat* journey

حقیقت *haqiqat* truth

A few pairs exist, each word usually having its own meaning:

اراده *erāde* will, wish

ارادت *erādat* sincerity

A few of these words make adverbs (see 7/2), all with the ending تاً... -*atan* (1/23), irrespective of the spelling of the noun:

قاعدتاً *qā'edatan* as a rule

حقیقتاً *haqiqatan* in truth

but see 7/2 also for the more common Persian adverbial phrases made from such words.

In a few clerical titles, the original Arabic spelling ة is found as well as Persian spelling with ت :

حجت الاسلام\حجة الاسلام *hajatoleslām* Hajatulislam
آیت الله\آیة الله *āyatollāh* Ayatollah

5 . قابل *qābele* and غیر *qeire*

The Arabic word قابل *qābel* 'able' is used together with some Arabic verbal nouns (10/3 above) to form compound adjectives corresponding to English adjectives ending in '-able', -'ible', 'worthy' and the like. The two words are connected with *ezāfe* (see 3/5, also Appendix II):

توجه *tavajjoh* attention	قابل توجه *qābele tavajjoh* notable, noteworthy, interesting
قبول *qabul* acceptance	قابل قبول *qābele qabul* acceptable
استفاده *estefāde* utilisation	قابل استفاده *qābele estefāde* utilisable
تجدید *tajdid* renewal	منابع قابل تجدید *manābe'e qābele tajdid* renewable resources

The Arabic word غیر *qeir* 'other' is used to negate some adjectives (including compound adjectives) taken from Arabic. It is followed by *ezāfe*:

رسمی *rasmi* official	غیر رسمی *qeire rasmi* unofficial
	غیر قابل قبول *qeire qābele qabul* unacceptable

6 . Definite article

Unlike Persian, Arabic has a definite article ...الـ *al-*. As used in Arabic, it mostly translates into English as 'the'; but in the Arabic phrases or compound words used in Persian this meaning is largely lost. The Arabic article is a prefix, attached to the word which it makes definite. The only things we need to know about it are how to spell it and pronounce it.

Its spelling never changes; it is always written ...الـ *alef-lām-*, and is always joined to the next word.

The general rule for its pronunciation is that it is never stressed, and does not affect the stress of the word to which it is attached. Further details concerning its pronunciation are given below.

Pronunciation of the ﺍ *alef.* The *alef* of the article is normally pronounced *a-*, but sometimes the vowel may become *o-* or *e-*:

الآن *alắn ‹alón›* now

فوق العاده *fouqal'ắde/fouqol'ắde* exceptional(ly)

بالأخره\بالاخره *belaxeré* (not *[bā-]*) finally

فى الفور *felfóur* immediately

Most such expressions have two or more words in Arabic, but all are best learned and transcribed as single words for our purposes.

Pronunciation of the ﻝ *lām.* The *lām* of the article is pronounced as *l* before most letters, as in the examples given above. But before any letter representing one of the sounds *t*, *d*, *r*, *s*, *š*, *z* or *n** the *l* of the article is not pronounced; instead that first following letter is doubled in pronunciation:

الساعه\الساعت *assā'é/assā'át/assāé/assāát* now

* The sounds are easily remembered. They are those produced with the tip or near-tip of the tongue, as is *l* itself.

Finally note the spelling of the Arabic word الله *allāh* 'God' (which incorporates a definite article), found in names and set expressions:

عزيز الله *azizollắh* Azizollah (name)

مسجد شيخ لطف الله *masjede šeix lotfollắh* the Sheikh Lotfollah mosque (in Isfahan)

الحمد لله *alhamdolellắh* praise be to God

ان شاء الله\انشاالله *enšā'allắh/enšallắh* perhaps

بسم الله *besmellắh* in the name of God

11. Wordbuilding

1. General

Much Persian vocabulary consists of base words which are expanded, with a consequent change of meaning and/or grammatical function, by adding prefixes, suffixes or middle parts, or by adding other words to form compounds; or by a combination of these devices. A base word itself may already be a derivative or a compound. Not all compound words are written as one word.

2. Derived and compound nouns

Prefixes. The prefix ...هم *ham* indicates 'together':

کار *kār* work	همکار *hamkār* colleague
شهر *šahr* town	همشهری *hamšahri* fellow-townsman
سایه *sāye* shade	همسایه *hamsāye* neighbour
بازی *bāzi* game	همبازی *hambāzi* playmate
درد *dard* pain	همدرد *hamdard* fellow-sufferer
راه *rāh* road	همراه *hamrāh* travelling companion

Suffixes. The following suffixes are added to make nouns:

- ی... *í*. This suffix, which always takes the stress of the word, is added to adjectives and to nouns denoting persons, to make abstract nouns or nouns of activity. This is the most productive noun suffix:

زود *zud* fast, soon	زودی *zudí* promptness
تند *tond* fast, brusque	تندی *tondí* speed, brusqueness
بزرگ *bozorg* big	بزرگی *bozorgi* size, greatness
راست *rāst* straight, right	راستی *rāsti* straightness, rightness
سفید *sefid* white	سفیدی *sefidi* whiteness
سخت *saxt* hard	سختی *saxti* hardship

189

سنگین *sangin* heavy   سنگینی *sangini* weight, gravity

هماهنگ *hamāhang* harmonious   هماهنگی *hamāhangi* harmony

مرد *mard* man   مردی *mardi* manliness

دوست *dust* friend   دوستی *dusti* friendship

همکار *hamkār* colleague   همکاری *hamkāri* cooperation

آشپز *āšpaz* cook   آشپزی *āšpazi* cookery

نقاش *naqqāš* painter   نقاشی *naqqāši* (act of) painting

Sometimes the base word is itself a compound (see under 'Compounds' later in this paragraph), whose elements may be written separately. An abstract noun derived from such a word is then also written as separate elements, the suffix being added at the end of the whole word as usual:

حق شناس *haq šenās* grateful   حق شناسی *haq šenāsi* gratitude

حق ناشناس *haq nāšenās* ungrateful   حق ناشناسی *haq nāšenāsi* ingratitude

زمین شناس *zamin šenās* geologist   زمین شناسی *zamin šenāsi* geology

After a base word ending in ا... *ā* or و... *u*, the suffix is spelt یی...; we also encounter the older spelling ئی... :

دانا *dānā* wise   دانایی *dānāi* wisdom

راستگو *rāstgu* truthful   راستگویی *rāstgui* truthfulness

A silent final ه (see 1/15) becomes گ before the ی... -*í* is added. This group includes participles, see 5/20:

گرسنه *gorosne* hungry   گرسنگی *gorosnegi* hunger

بسته *baste* tied, closed   بستگی *bastegi* connexion

خسته *xaste* tired   خستگی *xastegi* fatigue

بچه *bacce* child   بچگی *baccegi* childhood

نماینده *namāyande* representative   نمایندگی *namāyandegi* representation

This suffix can also indicate a place of activity:

کتابفروشی *ketābforuši*
bookshop

کتابفروش *ketābforuš*
bookseller

شهربانی *šahrbāni*
police headquarters

شهربان *šahrbān*
police chief

It also occurs in a few compounds with the present stem of
a verb (5/10), where there is no base word:

نامنویسی *nāmnevisi* registration

وزن کشی *vazn kaši* weighing

The various uses of the suffix ی... *-i* are summarised in
Appendix III.

- ش... *-éš* (یش... *-yéš* after a vowel). This suffix is added to
  some present stems of verbs to make a noun of activity. It
  takes the stress of the word:

کوشش *kušeš*
effort

کوشیدن کوشـ... *kušidan kuš-*
to strive

آموزش *āmuzeš*
learning

آموختن آموز... *āmuxtan āmuz-*
to learn

دانش *dāneš*
knowledge

دانستن دانـ... *dānestan dān-*
to know

ورزش *varzeš*
sport

ورزیدن ورز... *varzidan varz-*
to exercise

سوزش *suzeš*
burning

سوختن سوز... *suxtan suz-*
to burn

آزمایش *āzmāyeš*
experiment

آزمودن آزما... *āzmudan āzmā-*
to experiment

نمایش *namāyeš*
show

نمودن نما... *namudan namā-*
to show

پالایش\پالش
pālāyeš/pāleš refining

پالودن پالا... *pāludan pālā-*
to refine

فرمایش *farmāyeš*
command

فرمودن فرما... *farmudan farmā-*
to command

- A few nouns of activity are formed with the suffix ار... *-ắr*,
  added to the short infinitive (5/2) of a verb. The suffix
  takes the stress of the word:

191

رفت *raft* to go   رفتار *raftār* behaviour

گفت *goft* to say   گفتار *goftār* talk

دید *did* to see   دیدار *didār* view, meeting

- A few nouns of quality are made with the suffix ...ا *-ā́*, which is stressed:

گرم *garm* warm   گرما *garmā* warmth

پهن *pahn* wide   پهنا *pahnā* width

سرد *sard* cold   سرما *sarmā* cold (م ← د)

- Two suffixes indicating place. Both take the stress:

- ...ستان *-estā́n* (*-stā́n* after a vowel) indicates a big place, and is often used for countries or regions. Any final ...ی *-i* on the base word is dropped before suffixing; some words undergo other vowel changes:

شهر *šahr* city   شهرستان *šahrestān* county

انگلیسی *englisi* English, British   انگلستان *englestān* England, Britain

عرب *arab* Arab   عربستان *arabestān* Arabia

هندی *hendi* Indian   هندوستان *hendustān* India

مجار *majār* Hungarian   مجارستان *majārestān* Hungary

بیمار *bimār* sick   بیمارستان *bimārestān* hospital

- ...گاه *-gā́h* indicates a place where an activity is pursued:

دانش *dāneš* knowledge   دانشگاه *dānešgāh* university

آزمایش *āzmāyeš* experiment   آزمایشگاه *āzmāyešgāh* laboratory

بودن باش... *budan bāš-* to be   باشگاه *bāšgāh* club

نمایشگاه *namāyešgāh* نمایش *namāyeš*
exhibition   show

فرودگاه *forudgāh* فرود *forud*
airport   down(wards)

فروشگاه *forušgāh* فروختن فروش... *foruxtan foruš-*
stores   to sell

ایستگاه *istgāh* ایستادن ایست... *istādan ist-*
station, stop   to stop

پالایشگاه\پالشگاه پالودن پالا... *pāludan pālā-*
pālāyešgāh/pālešgāh refinery   to refine

- Three suffixes indicating agents:

  - بان...‏ *-bấn* (stressed) and چی...‏ *-ci* (unstressed). The latter is from Turkish '-çi', and is colloquial:

باغ *bāq* garden   باغبان *bāqbān* gardener

در *dar* door   دربان *darbān* doorman

پاس *pās* watch   پاسبان *pāsbān* policeman

شهر *šahr* city   شهربان *šahrbān* police chief

کشتی *kašti* ship   کشتیبان *kaštibān* captain

تلفن *telefon* telephone   تلفنچی *telefonci* telephonist

تفنگ *tofang* rifle   تفنگچی *tofangci* rifleman

پست *post* post, mail   پستچی *postci* postman

  - گر...‏ *-gar* and its variants کار...‏ *-kār*, گار...‏ *-gār*:

کار *kār* work   کارگر *kārgar* workman

درو *derou* harvest   دروگر *derougar* harvester

آهن *āhan* iron   آهنگر *āhangar* blacksmith

زر *zar* gold   زرگر *zargar* goldsmith

خدمت *xedmat* service   خدمتکار *xedmatkār* servant

آموختن آموز... *āmuxtan āmuz-*
to teach   آموزگار *āmuzgār* teacher

- Diminutives are forms indicating smallness, or, by association, endearment or denigration. They are formed by suffixing چه...‏ *-cé* (with silent ه) to nouns denoting things, or ك...‏ *-ák* to nouns in general. Both suffixes are stressed:

193

دریا *daryā* sea   دریاچه *daryāce* lake

کتاب *ketāb* book   کتابچه *ketābce* booklet, notebook

دیگ *dig* pot, pan   دیگچه *digce* small pot, saucepan

دختر *doxtar* girl   دخترك *doxtarak* little girl

پسر *pesar* boy   پسرك *pesarak* little boy

مرغ *morq* chicken   مرغک *morqak* chick

چهار *cahār* four   چارك *cārak* (for *[cahārak]*) quarter

سرخ *sorx* red   سرخک *sorxak* measles

- The stressed suffix ه... *-é* often indicates a measure:

دست *dast* hand   دسته *dasté* handful, bunch

هفت *haft* seven   هفته *hafte* week

نیم *nim* half (adjective) نیمه *nime* half (noun)

شمردن شمار... *šomordan šomār-* شماره *šomāre*
to count   number

Compounds. Important forms of compound nouns are shown below.

- Many compounds denoting agents (persons or things) are made with the present stem of an appropriate verb:

پختن پز... *poxtan paz-* to cook

آشپز *āšpaz* cook

فروختن فروش... *foruxtan foruš-* to sell

کتابفروش *ketābforuš* bookseller

میوه فروش *miveforuš* fruitseller

قالی فروش *qāli foruš* carpet dealer

سبزی فروش *sabzi foruš* greengrocer

داشتن دار... *dāštan dār-* to have

سردار *sardār* commander

کتابدار *ketābdār* librarian

حسابدار *hesābdār* accountant

برخاستن خیز... *bar xāstan xiz-* to rise

زودخیز *zudxiz* early riser

194

شستن شو... *šostan šu-* to wash

رختشو *raxtšu* launderer

باختن باز... *bāxtan bāz-* to forfeit

سرباز *sarbāz* soldier

کردن کن... *kardan kon-* to make

پاک کن *pāk kon* eraser

خشک کن *xošk kon* blotter, drier

رفتن روب... *roftan rub-* to sweep

مین روب *min rub* minesweeper

شناختن شناس... *šenāxtan šenās-* to know

زمین شناس *zamin šenās* geologist

نوشتن نویس... *neveštan nevis-* to write

تاریخ نویس *tārix nevis* historian

- Many nouns showing where an activity takes place are compounded with خانه *xāne* 'house':

آشپز *āšpaz* cook   آشپزخانه *āšpazxāne* kitchen

مهمان *mehmān* guest   مهمانخانه *mehmānxāne* guesthouse

کتاب *ketāb* book   کتابخانه *ketābxāne* library

سرباز *sarbāz* soldier   سربازخانه *sarbāzxāne* barracks

چای *cāi* tea   چایخانه *cāixāne* teashop

قهوه *qahve* coffee   قهوه خانه *qahvexāne* coffeeshop

مریض *mariz* sick   مریضخانه *marizxāne* hospital

دوا* *davā* ⎫ medicine   دواخانه *davāxāne* ⎫ pharmacy
دارو* *dāru* ⎭   داروخانه *dāruxāne* ⎭

* دوا(خانه) *davā* and *davāxāne* are the popular terms; دارو(خانه) *dāru* and *dāruxāne* are the official terms.

- Compounds exist formed from two nouns either juxtaposed, or connected with the *ezāfe* (see 3/5):

juxtaposed: صاحبخانه *sāhebxāne* landlord

پدرزن *pedarzan* (husband's) father-in-law

روزنامه *ruznāme* newspaper

with *ezāfe:* ميز تحرير *mize tahrir* desk

اطاق خواب *otāqe xāb* bedroom

دستور زبان *dasture zabān* grammar

دستور جلسه *dasture jalase* agenda

راه آهن *rāhe āhan* railway

- Some useful compounds denoting intense activity have been formed with redoubled verb stems (past or present, or mixed). Since these are 'petrified' formations, i.e. we do not make new ones, the words are most easily learned as items of vocabulary:

گفتن گو... *goftan gu-* to say   گفتگو *goftogu* conversation

جستن جو... *jostan ju-* to seek   جستجو *jostoju* search

شستن شو... *šostan šu-* to wash   شستشو *šostošu* washing

آمد *āmad* came, شد *šod* became   آمدوشد *āmadošod* traffic

Whether the compound is written as one word or more, each element retains its spelling, even if the rule given in 1/21 is apparently breached:

یاد *yād* memory, داشت *dāšt* to have

یادداشت *yāddāšt* memorandum, note

کباب فروشی *kabābforuši* Kebab stall

3. Derived and compound adjectives

The term *adjective* here includes participles (5/20) used as adjectives.

Prefixes. The most important adjectival prefix is the negative prefix ...نا *nā-*, added to an adjective, a noun, a phrase or verbal part:

راحت	*rāhat* comfortable	ناراحت	*nārāhat* uncomfortable
درست	*dorost* correct	نادرست	*nādorost* incorrect
پخته	*poxte* mature	ناپخته	*nāpoxte* immature
خوش	*xoš* well	ناخوش	*nāxoš* unwell
جور	*jur* sort	ناجور	*nājur* inappropriate
امید	*omid* hope	ناامید*	*nāomid* hopeless
حق	*haq* right (noun)	ناحق	*nāhaq* unjust
چیز	*ciz* thing	ناچیز	*nāciz* worthless
رسیدن رسـ...	*rasidan ras-* to arrive	نارس	*nāras* unripe
بودن باشـ...	*budan bāš-* to be	نابود	*nābud* nonexistent
حق‌شناس	*haq šenās* grateful	حق ناشناس	*haq nāšenās* ungrateful

* also commonly نومید *numid*

Suffixes. Suffixes added to make adjectives include:

- ی... *í*. This suffix, which always takes the stress of the word, makes adjectives from nouns. It is added in the same way as are the noun *-i* suffixes (11/2 above), except when added to a few base words ending in silent ه (1/15); see * at the end of this indent. This is the most productive adjectival suffix. Adjectives formed in this way are also used, where appropriate, as nouns with a meaning different from the base noun.

ایران	*irán* Iran	ایرانی	*iraní* Iranian
فارس	*fārs* Fars (province)	فارسی	*fārsí* Persian
آلمان	*ālmān* Germany	آلمانی	*ālmāni* German

ایل *il* tribe		ایلی *ili* tribal	
فرهنگ *farhang* culture		فرهنگی *farhangi* cultural	
ادب *adab* literature		ادبی *adabi* literary	
اختیار *extiār* choice		اختیاری *extiāri* optional	
روغن *rouqan* oil		روغنی *rouqani* oily	
چوب *cub* wood		چوبی *cubi* wooden	
پا *pā* foot		پایی *pāi* foot-driven	
بالا *bālā* top, upper part		بالایی *bālāi* upper	
هفته *hafte* week		هفتگی *haftegi* weekly	
خانه *xāne* house		خانگی *xānegi* domestic	

With a base noun taken from Arabic and ending in ت... -*at* or -*e* + silent ه , that ending is usually dropped before the suffix is added:

ملت *mellat* nation		ملی *melli* national	
نسبت *nesbat* relation(ship)		نسبی *nesbi* relative	
اداره *edāre* administration		اداری *edāri* administrative	
اضافه *ezāfe* addition		اضافی *ezāfi* additional	
but: راحت *rāhat* comfort(able)		صندلی راحتی *sandaliye rāhati* easy chair	

The suffix can be added to a long infinitive (5/2), giving it the meaning 'worthy of' or 'capable of':

دیدنی *didani* worth seeing

خوردنی *xordani* edible

دوست داشتنی *dust dāštani* likeable

* The suffix ی... -*í* is added as ای... (not گی... -*egi*) after a small number of nouns ending in -*e* + silent ه:

لوله *lule* tube		لوله‌ای *luleí* tubular	
پنبه *pambe* cotton		پنبه‌ای *pambei* (made of) cotton	

The uses of the suffix ی... -*i* are summarised in Appendix III.

- The stressed suffixes م... -*óm* and مین... -*omín* make ordinal numbers. The stressed suffix ه... -*é* makes adjectives from some numerical expressions. These derivatives are explained in 9/3, 6.

- Other adjectival suffixes exist, all of them 'petrified', i.e. of limited application which we cannot extend. Two worth noting are **ا...** *-ā́* added to the present stem of a few verbs (5/10), and **مند...** *-mánd* added to nouns, showing a characteristic trait. Both suffixes are stressed:

    دانستن دانـ... *dānestan dān-* to know   **دانا** *dānā* wise

    توانستن توانـ... *tavānestan tavān-* can   **توانا** *tavānā* powerful

    داشتن دار... *dāštan dār-* to have   **دارا***** *dārā* rich

    دولت *doulat* wealth   **دولتمند** *doulatmand* wealthy

    * most commonly used in a possessive structure (3/5), to express 'possessing':

    شخصی دارای نفوذ زیاد *šaxsi dārāye nofuze ziād*
    a person of/having/possessing great influence

    Words with these and other petrified suffixes are usually most easily learnt as items of vocabulary.

Compounds. Two important forms of compound adjectives are shown below.

- Many adjectives are formed by combining nouns, simple adjectives, numbers or verbal parts:

    چهارپا *cahārpā* four-footed
    تیزپا *tizpā* fleet-footed
    فارسی‌زبان *fārsi zabān* Persian-speaking
    گلرنگ *golrang* rose-coloured
    سنگدل *sangdel* hard-hearted
    دلتنگ *deltang* sad
    راستگو *rāstgu* truthful
    نشاط آور *nešāt āvar* pleasant
    حق شناس *haq šenās* grateful
    جهاندیده *jahāndide* experienced

- Compounds can be made with a preposition and a noun;

the commonest prepositions used are با *bā* 'with' and بی *bi* 'without'. بی in such compounds is often written joined to the base word:

هوش *huš* intelligence   باهوش *bāhuš* intelligent

معنی *ma'ni/ma'nā* meaning   بامعنی *bāma'ni/bāma'nā* significant

فهم *fahm* understanding   بی‌فهم\بیفهم *bi fahm/bifahm* stupid

صدا *sedā* noise   بی‌صدا *bi sedā* noiseless

Whether the compound is written as one word or more, each element retains its spelling, even if the rule given in 1/21 is apparently breached:

پر *por* full, رنگ *rang* colour

پررنگ *porrang* brightly coloured

See 3/9, 10 for the comparative and superlative of derived and compound adjectives.

See 10/5 for the formation of compound adjectives using the Arabic words قابل *qābel* and غیر *qeir*.

4 . Derived verbs

Verbs derived from nouns. A few verbs are derived from simple nouns. The derived long infinitive (5/2) ends in ...یدن *-idan*, and the present stem (5/10) is regular:

ترس *tars* fear   ترسیدن ترس... از *tarsidan tars- az* to fear

دزد *dozd* thief   دزدیدن دزد... *dozdidan dozd-* to steal

نام *nām* name   نامیدن نام... *nāmidan nām-* to name, to call

فهم *fahm* understanding   فهمیدن فهم... *fahmidan fahm-* to understand

خواب *xāb* sleep   خوابیدن خواب... *xābidan xāb-* to sleep

Causative verbs. Examine the English sentences, arranged in pairs:

200

The tree <u>is falling</u>. The gardener <u>is felling</u> the tree.

The plot <u>failed</u>. The police <u>foiled</u> the plot.

In each pair, the second sentence contains a *causative* verb: 'to fell' is to cause something to fall; 'to foil' is to cause something to fail. The causative verb makes its direct object (see 5/6) perform the action indicated.

Persian has a few important causative verbs; their long infinitive is derived from the base verb on the formula

<u>present stem + ...اندن\...انیدن- *-āndan/-ānidan*</u>

The present stem of the causative is regular.

سوختن سوز... *suxtan suz-* to burn/be on fire

سوزاندن سوزانـ... *suzāndan suzān-* to burn/set on fire

رسیدن رسـ... *rasidan ras-* to arrive

رساندن\رسانیدن رسانـ... *rasān(i)dan rasān-* to deliver

ترسیدن ترسـ... از *tarsidan tars- az* to fear

ترساندن\ترسانیدن ترسانـ... *tarsān(i)dan tarsān-* to frighten

گشتن\گردیدن گرد... *gaštan/gardidan gard-* to turn

گرداندن گردانـ... *gardāndan gardān-* to (make) turn

A few verbs have lost a syllable in the process:

رفتن رو... *raftan rav-* to go

راندن (برای [رواندن]) رانـ... *rāndan rān-* to drive (for [رواندن])

نشستن نشینـ... *nešastan nešin-* to sit

نشاندن (برای [نشیناندن]) نشانـ... *nešāndan nešān-* to seat (for [نشیناندن])

The verb گذشتن گذر... از *gozaštan gozar- az* 'to pass' is a special case. It has the following derived forms:

- one regular causative

گذراندن گذرانـ... *gozarāndan gozarān-* to pass (time etc.)

- two irregular causatives

گذاشتن گذار... *gozāštan gozār-* ⎫
گذاردن گذار... *gozārdan gozār-* ⎬ to put, to allow ⎭

Compound verbs are studied in 5/29 and 30.

12. Polite Forms

1. General

Persian has certain language forms which are used by all speakers to show respect, or at least to avoid sounding too familiar. We can call these 'polite forms'. This does not mean that what is called 'everyday speech' in this book is impolite; it is only less deferential. This chapter shows the most frequent polite forms. Colloquial pronunciation (see 2/6) can be used with polite forms.

2. Pronouns

The following polite pronoun variants are in common use:

- 'I'. Referring to oneself, بنده *bande* is used instead of من *man*. The verb stays in the من form:

  بنده نمی‌دانم. *bande nemi dānam ‹nemi dunam›.*
  I don't know.

- 'You'. See 4/2, second indent, explaining the widespread use of the plural شما *šomā* for 'you' in the singular. This is part of everyday speech. A deferential form for 'you' is جناب عالی *janābe āli*. Its verb stands in the شما form:

  جناب عالی وقت دارید؟ *janābe āli vaqt dārid?*
  Have you got time?

- 'He', 'she', 'they'. See 4/2, third indent. In everyday speech 'they' is آنها *ānhā ‹onhā›*. In polite speech the formal plural pronoun ایشان *išān ‹išon›* 'they' is used both for the singular 'he', 'she' and for the plural 'they'. Its verb agrees, i.e. goes into the plural.

  Everyday: او کجاست؟ *u kojāst?* Where is he/she?
  آنها کجا هستند؟ *ānhā ‹onhā› kojā hastand?*
  Where are they?
  Polite: ایشان کجا هستند؟ } { Where is he/she?
  išān ‹išon› kojā hastand? } { Where are they?

3 . Plural for singular

The second and third indents of 12/2 above examine the use of plural pronouns with plural verbs.

A verb with a singular noun as subject is also commonly made plural in polite language. The noun subject remains singular:

برادرتان هنوز نیامده اند. *barādaretān hanuz nayāmade and.*
Your brother has not come yet.

خانم هستند؟ *xānom hastand?* Is madame (in)?

4 . Verbs

There are in common use various polite alternatives for everyday verbs.

The following are used in the شما or ایشان persons, i.e. for the person(s) spoken to or the person(s) spoken about respectively:

- for the everyday بودن باش... *budan bāš-* to be (in a place):

  تشریف داشتن دار... *tašrif dāštan dār-*
  ('to have one's honour')

  آیا جناب عالی دیروز تشریف داشتید؟ *āyā janābe āli diruz tašrif dāštid?* Were you (there) yesterday?

  for آمدن آ... *āmadan ā-* to come:

  تشریف آوردن آور... *tašrif āvordan āvar-*
  ('to bring one's honour')

  ایشان تشریف نیاوردند. *išān tašrif nayāvordand.*
  He/She/They didn't come.

  for رفتن رو... *raftan rav-* to go:

  تشریف بردن بر... *tašrif bordan bar-*
  ('to take one's honour')

  حالا تشریف می برید؟ حیف است. *hālā tašrif mi barid? heif ast.* You're going now? That's a pity.

- for گفتن گو... *goftan gu-* to say:

  فرمودن فرما... *farmudan farmā-* ('to command')

  چه فرمودید خانم؟ *ce farmudid xānom?*
  What did you say, ma'am?

for ...خواه خواستن *xāstan xāh-* to want, to request:

میل داشتن دار... *meil dāštan dār-*

میل فرمودن فرما... *meil farmudan farmā-* }
('to be inclined to')

برای شام چه میل دارید\می‌فرمایید؟ *barāye šām ce meil dārid/mi farmāid?* What would you like for dinner?

for ...فهم فهمیدن *fahmidan fahm-* to understand:

ملتفت شدن شو... *moltafet šodan šav-*
('to be attentive')

ملتفت شدید چرا اینطورگفتند؟ *moltafet šodid cerā intour goftand?* Did you understand why they said that ('thus')?

- In compound verbs (5/29) formed with کردن کن... *kardan kon-* and with certain other base verbs, the verbal part is replaced by ...فرمودن فرما *farmudan farmā-* 'to command' in polite speech:

مدیر دیروز تلفن فرمودند (= تلفن کرد). *modir diruz telefon farmudand (= telefon kard).* The director telephoned yesterday.

کی حرکت فرمودید (= حرکت کردید)؟ *kei harakat farmudid (= harakat kardid)* When did you leave?

...ایشان اجازه نفرمودند (= او اجازه نداد) که *išān ejāze nafarmudand (= u ejāze nadād) ke ...* He/She did not permit...

Speaking for oneself or a group, we can replace ...گو گفتن *goftan gu-* 'to say' with the common polite form ...عرض کردن کن *arz kardan kon-* ('to petition'):

...به ایشان عرض کردم که *be išān arz kardam ke ...* I told him/her that ...

The present-tense form ... عرض می‌کنم که *arz mi konam ke ...* is also used to mean 'If I may say so, ...', 'With respect, ...':

عرض می‌کنم که اینطور نیست. *arz mi konam ke intour nist.* With respect, it isn't like that.

See 5/29. For all the compound verbs shown above, the subjunctive (5/16) and imperative (5/18) usually have the

...بیـ...\ـبـ *be-/bi-* prefix:

لطفًا ساعت دو تشریف بیاورید. *lotfan sā'ate do tašrif biāvarid.*
Please come at two o'clock.

عرض می‌کنم که فردا تلفن بفرمایید.
arz mi konam ke fardā telefon befarmāid.
Perhaps you could/May I suggest that you telephone tomorrow.

But rhetorical questions constructed with the subjunctive of these verbs usually have no subjunctive prefix:

چه عرض کنم؟ *ce arz konam?* What can I say?

5. Prepositions

In polite speech we often replace the prepositions به *be* 'to' or برای *barāye* 'for' with the noun خدمت *xedmat* 'service' with reference to the person(s) spoken to or the person(s) spoken about. This noun takes either the possessive *ezāfe* (3/5) or a possessive-adjective suffix (3/11):

... خدمت وزیر عرض کردم که *xedmate vazir arz kardam ke ...*
I mentioned to the minister that ...

... نامه‌ای که خدمت شما\خدمتتان نوشتم
nāmei ke xedmate šomā/xedmatetān neveštam ...
The letter which I wrote to/for you ...

خدمت can also replace the preposition پیش *piše* 'to(wards)', in which case 'seeing' or 'visiting' is implied:

دیروز خدمتتان آمدند. *diruz xedmatetān āmadand.*
He/She/They came to see you yesterday.

6. Requesting and thanking

In polite speech as in everyday speech, we distinguish between the two expressions translated into English as 'please':

خواهش می‌کنم *xāheš mi konam*
('I request') (asking for something)

بفرمایید *befarmāid*
('Command') (offering something)

206

دو كيلو خواهش مى كنم. ‏ do kilo, xāheš mi konam.
Two kilos, please.

از اينجا بفرماييد. ‏ az injā befarmāid.
Please (come) this way.

خواهش مى كنم ‏ xāheš mi konam is also 'Don't mention it' or 'You're welcome', in response to an expression of thanks.

The expressions مرسى ‏ mersi and متشكرم ‏ motašakkeram 'Thank you', used in everyday speech, can become in polite speech ممنونم ‏ mamnunam 'I am grateful':

از التفات شما خيلى ممنونم. ‏ az eltefāte šomā xeili mamnunam.
I am very grateful for your kindness.

A still more polite formula of thanks is

مرحمتتان زياد (است). ‏ marhamatetān ziād (ast).
'Your kindness (is) great'.

207

Appendix I
Irregular present stems of verbs

See 5/10. Only commonly used verbs are listed below. Colloquial pronunciation (2/6) of present stems (and of three past stems) is shown in angular quotation marks ‹ ›. For brevity, the particle 'to' is omitted from the English infinitive.

آزمودن	āzmudan	آزما...	āzmā-	experiment
آفريدن	āfaridan	آفرين...	āfarin-	create
افزودن	afzudan	افزا...	afzā-	increase
آمدن	āmadan ‹umad-›	آ...	ā-*	come
آموختن	āmuxtan	آموز...	āmuz-	teach
آميختن	āmixtan	آميز...	āmiz-	mix
انداختن	andāxtan	انداز...	andāz-	throw
آوردن	āvordan/āvardan	آور...\آر...	āvar-/ār-	bring
آويختن	āvixtan	آويز...	āviz-	hang
باختن	bāxtan	باز...	bāz-	lose, forfeit
بايستن	bāyestan (defective)	بايد	bāyad**	must
بردن	bordan	بر...	bar-	carry, take away
بستن	bastan	بند...	band-	tie, close
بودن	budan	باش...	bāš-	be
پالودن	pāludan	پالا...	pālā-	refine, distil
پختن	poxtan	پز...	paz-	cook
پذيرفتن	paziroftan	پذير...	pazir-	receive
پرداختن	pardāxtan	پرداز...	pardāz-	pay
پيمودن	peimudan	پيما...	peimā-	measure
پيوستن	peivastan	پيوند...	peivand-	join
تافتن	tāftan	تاب...	tāb-	shine, twist
توانستن	tavānestan ‹tunest-›	توان...	tavān- ‹tun-›	can
جستن	jostan	جو...	ju-	look for

209

چیدن	cidan	چینـ...	cin-	collect, lay (table)
خاستن	xāstan	خیزـ...	xiz-	rise
خواستن	xāstan	خواهـ...	xāh-*	want
دادن	dādan	دهـ...	deh- ‹d-›	give
داشتن	dāštan	دارـ...	dār-	have
دانستن	dānestan ‹dunest-›	دانـ...	dān- ‹dun-›	know
دوختن	duxtan	دوزـ...	duz-	sew
دیدن	didan	بینـ...	bin-	see
رفتن	raftan	روـ...	rav- ‹r-›	go
رفتن	roftan	روبـ...	rub-	sweep
زدن	zadan	زنـ...	zan-	beat
ساختن	sāxtan	سازـ...	sāz-	make
سپردن	sepordan	سپارـ...	sepār-	entrust
شایستن	šāyestan (defective)	شاید	šāyad**	may
شدن	šodan	شوـ...	šav- ‹š-›	become
شستن	šostan	شوـ...	šu- ‹šur-›	wash
شکستن	šekastan	شکنـ...	šekan-	break
شمردن	šomordan	شمارـ...	šomār-	count
شناختن	šenāxtan	شناسـ...	šenās-	know
شنیدن	šenidan	شنوـ...	šenav-	hear
فرمودن	farmudan	فرماـ...	farmā-	command
فروختن	foruxtan	فروشـ...	foruš-	sell
فریفتن	fariftan	فریبـ...	farib-	deceive
فشردن	fešordan	فشارـ...	fešār-	press
کاشتن	kāštan	کارـ...	kār-	cultivate
کردن	kardan	کنـ...	kon-	do
کوفتن	kuftan	کوبـ...	kub-	pound
گذاشتن	gozāštan	گذارـ...	gozār- ‹zār-›	put
گذشتن	gozaštan	گذرـ...	gozar- ‹zar-›	pass
گرفتن	gereftan	گیرـ...	gir-	take
گشتن	gaštan	گردـ...	gard-	become, turn
گفتن	goftan	گوـ...	gu- ‹g-›	say

مردن mordan	میر... mir-	die
نشستن nešastan	نشین... nešin-	sit
نمودن namudan	نما... namā-	show
نوشتن neveštan	نویس... nevis-	write
یافتن yāftan	یاب... yāb-	find

* See 5/10 under 'Colloquial pronunciation'. In the colloquial present stem of آمدن āmadan, -āya becomes -ā-. In the colloquial present stem of خواستن xāstan, -āha becomes -ā-; see 5/19 under خواستن xāstan.

** باید\شاید bāyad/šāyad: Not the present stems, but the present 3rd person singular forms used for all persons. See 5/19.

Appendix II
اضافه *ezāfe*

1. General

The word اضافه *ezāfe* means 'addition' or 'supplement'. It is an important grammatical device, which takes the form of a suffix added to a word to show its relationship to the following word or words.

For clarity, the pronunciation of the *ezāfe* is printed bold in the transcription of the examples given below.

2. Writing and pronunciation

The *ezāfe* is never stressed, and never affects the stress of the word to which it is attached. It is written and pronounced as follows:

- when added after a consonant, it may be marked with the short vowel ... (*kasre* or *zir*, see 1/23); but as short vowels are very rarely marked, it is usually left unwritten in this position. It is pronounced -*e*:

  کتاب من *ketābe man* my book
  راه کاشان *rāhe kāšān* the Kashan road
  خانم عباسی *xanome abbāsi* Mrs Abbasi
  شهر قشنگ *šahre qašang* a/the beautiful city
  داخل پستخانه *dāxele postxāne* inside the post office
  خواندن این نامه *xāndane in nāme*
  (the) reading (of) this letter

- when added to silent ه (1/15), or after ی -*i*, it is usually left unwritten; after silent ه it may be marked with *hamze* over the ه. It is pronounced -*ye*:

  خانه او\خانهٔ او *xāneye u* his house
  میوه شیرین\میوهٔ شیرین *miveye širin* sweet fruit

  In this book the *hamze* is shown.

213

Formerly the spelling ئ... was also used optionally to show the *ezāfe* of *-iye*. We now leave the final ی... unmarked:

کشتی بادی (کشتیئ) *kaštiye bādi* sailing ('wind') boat

- when added after ا *-ā* or و *-u/ou*, it is written ی and pronounced *-ye*:

آقای هیوی *āqāye hayavi* Mr Hayavi

بچه های کوچك *baccehāye kucek* little children

بوی بد *buye bad* the bad smell

روی میز *ruye miz* on the table

جلوی ایستگاه *jelouye istgāh* in front of the station

3. Use

The *ezāfe* is used as follows. Full explanation is given in the paragraphs indicated:

- between nouns in the so-called possessive structure, and between certain nouns in apposition (3/5):

میز تحریر *mize tahrir* writing table

ماشین سفیر *māšine safir* the ambassador's car

آقای مشیری *āqāye moširi* Mr Moshiri

- between a noun and a following attributive adjective (3/8):

نیروی هوایی *niruye havāi* air force

- between noun and pronoun in possessive structure (3/11):

پیشنهاد شما *pišnehāde šomā* your proposal

- between a long infinitive and its direct object (5/2):

نوشتن تاریخ *neveštane tārix* history-writing

- between certain prepositions and the noun or pronoun which they govern (6/3):

زیر زمین *zire zamin* below the earth

برای آنها *barāye ānhā* for them

- between the elements of certain compound adjectives of Arabic origin (10/5):

غیر قابل قبول *qeire qābele qabul* unacceptable

214

Appendix III
Suffix ی... -*i*

1. General

The suffix ی... -*i* is the most versatile of the suffixes. It is examined in detail in the paragraphs referred to below. This Appendix summarises its various forms and uses. These split into two distinct groups.

2. Group 1

This group consists of two types, the *indefinite -i* and the *relative -i*. In both types the suffix has the following characteristics:

- It is unstressed, and does not affect the stress of the word.
- It is pronounced *i*.
- It is written:
  - after a consonant: ی... .
  - after ا, or و pronounced *u*: یی .
  - after silent ه (1/15): ای .
- It is added to the end of a noun or a noun-and-adjective expression.
- It is not added to a word already ending in ی... .
- When appropriate, it is added after a plural suffix, but before a definite direct-object suffix را *rā*.
- It is not found in combination with a possessive-adjective suffix (3/11).

The two types in the group are described respectively in paragraphs 3 and 4 below, with references for each example.

3. Indefinite ی... -*i*

See paragraph 2 above. The indefinite -*i* is added, in the manner described there:

215

- to a countable noun or noun-and-adjective expression:

  - to make it indefinite (i.e. to show that it is unidentified to at least one party of the dialogue):

$$\left.\begin{array}{l}
\text{كتابی } \textit{ketābi} \text{ (a/any/some) book} \\
\text{صدایی } \textit{sedāi} \text{ (a/any/some) sound} \\
\text{پارویی } \textit{pārui} \text{ (a/any/some) spade} \\
\text{کوزه ای } \textit{kuzei} \text{ (a/any/some) jug}
\end{array}\right\} 3/2$$

$$\left.\begin{array}{l}
\text{کتاب کوچکی } \textit{ketābe kuceki} \\
\text{کتابی کوچك } \textit{ketābi kucek}
\end{array}\right\} \left\{\begin{array}{l}
\text{a/any/some} \\
\text{small book}
\end{array}\right\} 3/8$$

چیزهایی *cizhāi* (any/some) things   3/4

کتابی را خرید. *ketābi rā xarid.*   3/3
He/She bought a (certain) book

  - after certain interrogative adjectives (3/13):

چه مردی؟ *ce mardi?* what man?

چطور مردی؟ *cetour mardi?* what kind of man?

  - with a negative verb, to express 'no', 'none', 'not any':

اشکالی نیست. *eškāli nist.* There is no difficulty.   3/14

کسی نیامد. *kasi nayāmad.* Nobody came.   4/10

- to any noun or noun-and adjective expression, in exclamations (8/16):

چه تکبری! *ce takabbori!* What arrogance!

چه اسبهای قشنگی! *ce asbhāye qašangi!*
What beautiful horses!

- to يك *yek* 'one' and to كم *kam* 'little', to make pronouns, and to كم also to make an adverb:

یکی از آنها *yeki az ānhā* one of them   9/2

کدام یکی؟ *kodām yeki?* which one?   3/13

کمی می خورد. *kami mi xorad.* He eats (a) little   4/10

کمی بهتر *kami behtar* a little better   7/2

4. Relative ی... -i

See paragraph 2 above. The relative -i is added, in the manner described there, to a noun or noun-and-adjective expression, or to the pronoun نها ānhā 'they/those', when one of these is the antecedent of an identifying relative (8/6):

شخصی که *šaxsi ke* the person who

نامه‌ای (را) که نوشتم *namei (rā) ke nevestam* the letter which I wrote

بچه‌هایی را که *baccehāi rā ke* the children whom

کتاب جدیدی که *ketābe jadidi ke* the new book which

این کتابی است که *in ketābi st ke* this is the book which

آنهایی که *ānhāi ke* they/those who

5 . Group 2

This group consists of two types, the *noun -i* and the *adjectival -i*. In both types the suffix changes the meaning and grammatical type of the word to which it is added. In both types the suffix has the following characteristics:

- It takes the stress of the word.
- It is written and pronounced:
  - after a consonant: ی... pronounced *-i*.
  - after ا, or و pronounced *u*: یی pronounced *-i*.
  - after silent ه (1/15) in Persian words: in almost all cases (and in all participles) the ه is dropped and the suffix takes the form گی... pronounced *-egi*. But see paragraph 7 below.
  - after words taken from Arabic and ending in silent ه, or in ت... *-at*: the last vowel and consonant are dropped and ی... pronounced *-i* is added to the preceding consonant.
- It is not added to a word already ending in ی... .

The two types in the group are described respectively in paragraphs 6 and 7 below, with references for each example.

6 . Noun ‫ی‬... -*i*

See 11/2. Noun -*i* is added, in the manner described in paragraph 5 above, to an adjective or to a noun denoting a person, to make an abstract noun or a noun denoting an activity or the place where an activity is pursued. The base adjective or noun may be a participle (5/20):

بزرگی *bozorgi* greatness, size   تنهایی *tanhāi* solitude

راستگویی *rāstgui* truthfulness   خستگی *xastegi* fatigue

دوستی *dusti* friendship   رانندگی *rānandegi* driving

آشپزی *āšpazi* cookery   کتابفروشی *ketābforuši* bookshop

7 . Adjectival ‫ی‬... -*i*

See 11/3. Adjectival -*i* is added, in the manner described in paragraph 5 above, to a noun to make the corresponding adjective. The noun may be a long infinitive (5/2):

نسبی *nesbi* relative   ایرانی *irāni* Iranian

چوبی *cubi* wooden   پایی *pāi* pedal-, foot-

هفتگی *haftegi* weekly   اداری *edāri* administrative

خوردنی *xordani* edible   گفتنی *goftani* worth saying

In the case of a few adjectives made from native Persian nouns ending in silent ه (1/15), the ه... is retained and we add ای... pronounced -*i*:

کرایه ای *kerāyei* rented, for rent

Appendix IV
Definite direct-object suffix را *rā*

1. General

The use of the definite direct-object suffix را *rā* is explained in the
text where it arises. It is summarised here, with references, for
convenience. For the term *definite* see 3/2; for the term *direct object*
see 5/6.

2. Writing and pronunciation

The suffix را *rā* is almost always written detached from its base
word, even when that word ends in a joined letter (1/2):

شخص را *šaxs rā* the person

فراش را *farrāš rā* the office boy

مرد را *mard rā* the man

بچه را *bacce rā* the child

In older Persian we can find the suffix attached to its word when
the spelling permits it, especially after the pronouns این *in* 'this', آن
ān 'it/that', and ایشان *išān* 'he/she/they' (4/3):

این را (اینرا) for *in rā* it/this

With the pronoun مرا *marā* 'me' the suffix is always joined; with
the pronoun ترا *torā* 'you' it is also joined, though تورا (same
pronounciation) is also found. See paragraph 3, last indent,
below.

The suffix را is never stressed, and never affects the stress of its
base word. It is pronounced colloquially ‹ro› or ‹o› after a
consonant, and ‹ro› after a vowel:

این شخص را ‹in šaxs ro/in šaxs o› this person

آن بچه ها را ‹un baccehā ro› those children

مرا *marā* 'me' is sometimes replaced colloquially by the form
‹máno›.

3. Use

The suffix marks the definite direct object (5/6) of a verb. It is added for this purpose, after any other suffixes which there may be:

- to a noun (3/3, 4) or a noun expression, i.e. an expression consisting of noun + noun (3/5), noun + adjective (3/8, 9), noun + possessive (3/11) or adjective + noun (3/8, 10, 12, 13, 14):

  معلم را ندیده اید؟ *mo'allem rā nadide id?*
  Have you not seen the teacher?

  فرهنگ فارسی را برده اند. *farhange fārsi rā borde and.*
  They have taken the Persian dictionary.

  دوچرخه‌ام را در بازار گم کردم. *docarxeam rā dar bāzār gom kardam.* I lost my bicycle in the market.

  دوچرخهٔ شما را نگرفته ام. *docarxeye šomā rā nagerefte am.* I have not taken your bicycle.

  این سندها را کجا پیدا کردید؟ *in sanadhā rā kojā peidā kardid?* Where did you find these documents?

  هر نامه را با دقت نگاه می‌کنند. *har nāme rā bā deqqat negāh mi konand.* They look at every letter carefully.

  کدام نقش را بیشتر دوست دارید؟ *kodām naqš rā bištar dust dārid?* Which design do you like more?

- to a noun or noun expression carrying the indefinite suffix ی... *-i* (see 3/2, 3), when the identity of the noun is known to one party:

  بالأخره چه فیلمی را دیدند؟ *belaxere ce filmi rā didand?*
  What film did they finally see?

  برای بچه ها دبیرستانی را انتخاب کرده اند.
  barāye baccehā dabirestāni rā entexāb karde and.
  They have chosen a secondary school for the children.

  Often this suggests the meaning of the English expression 'a certain ...':

فرشی را خریده اند. *farši rā xaride and.*

They have bought a (certain) carpet.

(one known to them but not necessarily to me)

- to a noun element of some compound verbs (5/29):

درس را نخوانده اند. *dars rā naxānde and.*

They have not studied the lesson.

- to a noun or noun expression which is the antecedent of an identifying relative clause (see 8/6), when either that noun or noun expression, or the relative pronoun که *ke* (or each one in turn) is the direct object of the verb in its own clause. In this use of را , the suffix is not obligatory; if it is used, it stands between the relative suffix ی... *-i* and the relative pronoun که *ke*. Examine three examples:

- شخصی (را) که زنگ می‌زد نمی‌شناسم.

šaxsi (rā) ke zang mi zad nemi šenāsam.

I don't know the person who was ringing.

(The antecedent شخص is the direct object of its own verb نمی‌شناسم in the main clause.)

- مسجدی (را) که دیدیم قشنگ است.

masjedi (rā) ke didim qašang ast.

The mosque which we saw is beautiful.

(The relative pronoun که *ke* is the direct object of its own verb دیدیم in the relative clause.)

- کتابی (را) که خریدم گم کرده ام.

ketābi (rā) ke xaridam gom karde am.

I have lost the book that I bought.

(The antecedent کتاب, and the relative pronoun که *ke*, are each in turn the direct object of their own verb.)

When را is added to a noun-and-adjective expression, it follows the whole expression: see examples under the first indent above.

- to the pronouns

  - من *man* I (← مرا *marā* me)   ما *mā* we
    تو *to* you (← ترا *torā* you)   شما *šomā* you
    او *u* he/she   آنها *ānhā* they
    آن *ān* it   ایشان *išān* they

    for which see 4/3; also 12/2 for ایشان .

  - مال من *māle man* mine (etc.), see 4/5.

  - این *in* this, آن *ān* that, اینها *inhā* these, آنها *ānhā* those,
    همین *hamin* the same/this very one, see 4/6.

  - کی *ki* who/whose, چه *ce* what, see 4/7.

  - خود *xod* oneself, خودم *xodam* myself (etc.), see 4/8.

  - همدیگر\یکدیگر *hamdigar/yekdigar* each other, see
    4/9.

  - هر کس *har kas* everyone, هر چیز\همه چیز\همه اش
    har ciz/hame ciz/hamaš everything, همه *hame* all (plural),
    see 4/10.

  - بنده *bande* I, جناب عالی *janābe āli* you, see 12/2.

When there are several direct objects of the same verb and the
objects are connected with و *va/o* 'and', the suffix را is put once,
after the last object:

پدر و پسر را دیدیم.   *pedar va pesar rā didim.*
We saw father and son.

من و ترا نمی‌شناسند.   *man o torā nemi šenāsand.*
They don't know you and me.

222

Index

References are to **chapter**/paragraph number or **appendix**/paragraph number. The sign → refers you to another entry in the index.